THE
SAKÉ
COMPANION

日本酒

THE
SAKÉ
COMPANION

A CONNOISSEUR'S GUIDE

BY JOHN GAUNTNER

RUNNING PRESS
PHILADELPHIA · LONDON

To Mayu.
'Nuff said.

Printed in China

9   8   7   6   5   4   3   2   1
Digit on the right indicates the number of this printing

Library of Congress Cataloging-in-Publication Number 00-131321

ISBN 0-7624-0804-9

Cover design by Terry Peterson
Interior design by Alicia Freile
Edited by Melissa Wagner
Typography: Fairfield, Franklin Gothic, and Serlio

This book may be ordered by mail from the publisher.
Please include $2.50 for postage and handling.
But try your bookstore first!

Running Press Book Publishers
125 South Twenty-second Street
Philadelphia, Pennsylvania 19103-4399

Visit us on the web!
www.runningpress.com

ACKNOWLEDGMENTS

Indeed it is difficult to thank all of those along the strange but interesting path that has led to the manifestation of this book. First, thanks should go to Masao Anzai, who introduced me to the world of good saké all those years ago. Next, thanks to my friend Rick Warm for being the first to encourage me to write about saké. The many other teachers and friends include Philip Harper of Umenoyado for more than he may be aware of—or willing to take credit for; Haruo Matsuzaki for untellable hours of friendship and teaching; everyone from the Bushukai in Hachioji; and Jiro Shinoda for sharing wisdom and encouragement. Also, special thanks to Brad Glosserman for getting the whole writing thing started, and Mark Thompson and Yamaguchi-san at the *Japan Times* for keeping it rolling all these years. Gratitude goes out to Grif Frost of SakéOne for encouragement and support. Thanks, too, to Bryan Harrell for editorial and content advice as well as aiding and abetting in empirical research at Sasagin. Not to be forgotten is my good friend Mark Schumacher for giving me a saké cyber-presence second to none. Finally, thanks to my family for patiently allowing me to be where I am, and to my wife Mayuko for her cheerleading and love.

The Publisher would like to thank Ambassador Wines and Spirits, 1020 2nd Ave., New York, New York, for providing the bottles of sake shown in the cover photographs and the photographs which appear on pages two and six.

CONTENTS

Hokkaidō

Aomori

Akita   Iwate

Yamagata   Miyagi

Niigata

Fukushima

Ishikawa   Tochigi
Gumma   Ibaraki
Toyama
Nagano   Chiba
Gifu   Tokyo
Fukui   Kanagawa

Hyōgo   Saitama
                Yamanashi
Tottori
                Shizuoka
Shimane   Aichi
Hiroshima   Mie
                Shiga
Yamaguchi   Nara
                Wakayama
Fukuoka   Ōsaka
Nagasaki
                Kyotō
Saga
Kumamoto   Tokushima
Ōita
                Kagawa
Kagoshima
                Okayama

                Kōchi
                Ehime
Miyazaki

Part I

THE STORY OF SAKÉ

Introduction

Saké has—until somewhat recently—been a fairly obscure beverage. Outside of Japan, it has long been viewed as more of a curiosity than a craft beverage. The fact that most restaurants served (as many still do) saké piping hot certainly did not help the situation. After all, how good could a scalding beverage be? Could something that assaults your taste buds with heat possibly warrant much attention?

Even within Japan, saké has been viewed, until recently, as something of an old codger's drink, devoid of style or class, and has not been embraced by the mainstream in its finer manifestations. Fortunately, all that is changing, and changing quickly.

Also known as *nihonshu*, or *seishu* in legalese, saké provides as much potential for outstandingly enjoyable gourmet appreciation as wine or any other fine beverage. Those that might disagree, regardless of their experience with other connoisseur's drinks, simply have not tasted enough good saké.

There are myriad reasons why saké has not become more familiar in the West. One reason is that truly good saké has been around on a large scale for only about thirty to forty years. Before then, it was more of a folk drink, produced on a small level for local consumption. To be sure, there has always been some super premium saké available, but for a long time it was somewhat hidden in the recesses, all but unknown in the face of the mass producers. Exposure to saké in the West was long limited to such mass-produced saké and the somewhat homogenized styles that result from nearly all large-scale production. As this mostly hot and often lifeless stuff was all that was available upon which to base an opinion, the image of saké remained confined to the lower echelons of fine beverage appreciation.

Language has, of course, also been a barrier. The Japanese and English languages are vastly different, and the different writing systems render saké labels indecipherable to the English language speaker, regardless of how beautiful they may be.

In spite of these barriers, the popularity of saké is now reaching a point where a whole world could soon open for consumers with an interest. More and more types, brands, and flavor profiles could soon become available, and with appropriate competition, consumer prices will decrease. In order for that to happen, saké appreciation in the West will need to achieve a critical mass. This will occur when enough discerning tasters see the potential and appeal of saké. It will take some effort on the part of consumers to create their own preferences by learning and remembering brands and flavors, provoking educated purchases. It will also require the effort of importers and producers, domestic and Japanese, to patiently and doggedly educate and market. Finally, it will call for effort on the part of the distribution industry to improve availability of good saké on a nationwide basis.

When this happens, consumer demand will cause the major barriers to fall. Prices will come down, availability will improve, and information will flow like. . . well, like saké. It is hoped that this book will contribute to this end.

A Brief History

Like the other fermented fruit and grain beverages of the world, saké was not so much developed as it was discovered. Around the third century, soon after wet rice cultivation began in Japan, rice that had been left out uncovered was exposed to natural, airborne, enzyme-producing spores. Yeast fell on the resulting moldy mash, and the resulting mixture was found to create a certain euphoria in those who consumed it. This in turn provoked enough curiosity that a more controlled process was eventually sought. People would save a bit of the mixture and combine it with more rice to make another "batch," similar to a sourdough starter. At this stage, saké was still more of a solid than a beverage, and was also relatively low in alcohol, since minimal yeast fell into the vats.

The first great milestone of Japan's long and winding history with saké was the establishment of a brewing department within the Imperial Palace in the former capital of Nara. By the beginning of the Heian Era (794-1192), commoners were feasting on slightly improved versions of this moldy mash, while the aristocracy had appointed a group of craftsmen to develop and brew several types of saké. These craftsmen produced at least fifteen varieties for occasions such as festivals and holidays, with a wide range of flavor profiles and brewing techniques. Some were sweet, some were heavy, and some were brewed specifically for their high alcohol content. Still others were flavored or colored. It was about this time that some saké began to be consumed warmed—likely an influence from China, where rice beverages were also being developed.

Outside the palace walls, there were about 180 independent brewers in the Kyoto area alone. Soon, saké breweries (today known as *kura*, or *sakagura*) began to flourish on the grounds of temples and shrines, with their plentiful supplies of land, rice, and industrious monks. As the economy began to stabilize, many brewing families also aligned themselves with such religious sites, in an effort to ensure their survival and prosperity. By the late fourteenth century, there was healthy competition among Kyoto brewers, then several hundred in number. Technical developments took place: a "starter" mash with an extremely high concentration of yeast cells was developed, as was the isolation of *kōji* spores (the mold that converts rice starch to sugar for fermentation).

As Japan entered civil war, and its capital moved to Kamakura and back, the fortunes of the saké world rose and fell accordingly. Still, the technology behind it continued to grow. Pasteurization came into use based on empirical observations, although it would be several hundred years before Louis Pasteur figured out why it worked. Texts from 1599 indicate that the three-stage brewing process used today had already been discovered. When white rice replaced brown rice in every step of the brewing process (as opposed to using unmilled rice in some steps), all the key elements of saké brewing as we know it today were in place.

Technical improvements continued over the next three hundred years. Most were the result of experience and the need to save time and manpower. As chemical analysis became possible, with more accurate measurements of temperature and other parameters, saké of consistently higher standards was produced.

Under the relatively stable reign of the Tokugawa regime, connoisseurs in Edo (present-day Tokyo) began to demand the finest saké available. Access to a seaport that provided easy shipping to Edo, combined with the discovery of excellent water for brewing, made Kobe a major brewing center, and it remains so today.

In 1871, just after the Meiji Restoration, which wrested power from the Tokugawa Shogunate and reinstated government under the Emperor, a law was passed allowing basically anyone who had the resources to begin brewing saké. Nearly thirty thousand breweries opened in one year, although many faded into oblivion as the government increased taxes on saké. By 1900, Japan was home to about eight thousand breweries. Many were operated by wealthy landowners, some of whom established saké breweries as a way to deal with excess rice, which could not be stored for long periods. Although the economic environment has changed drastically since then, many breweries are still owned by the same families that operated them centuries ago.

As the twentieth century began, brewing technology improved almost exponentially. The tax department of the Treasury Ministry established a saké brewing research institute in 1904, and three years later it held the first government-sponsored tasting competition for freshly brewed saké, a major industry event that still continues today. At the same time, a Central Brewers' Union began to provide pure yeast strains, many of which were isolated at the research centers which sprang up around the country. Soon, enamel-coated fermentation tanks replaced the cedar tanks that had been used for centuries. Massive improvements were also seen in rice-milling equipment, a deceptively important step in the brewing process.

World War II dealt a crushing blow to the saké industry, with almost half of the nearly seven thousand breweries forced to cease brewing. During the war, the process of adding alcohol to a fermenting saké mash, a practice which began around 1700, began to get a bit out of hand. Although this process had been discontinued both legally and in practice in the late 1800s, it was legalized again during the war to compensate for rice shortages. The use of flavoring combined with distilled alcohol allowed saké to be produced with less rice, and in some rare cases, none at all. Naturally, quality suffered, but the practice was never entirely discontinued even after the war ended. Later, adding small amounts of alcohol during fermentation was found to provide certain benefits to the flavor and fragrance, although, some would argue, at a price.

Gradually, the saké industry returned to its prewar production volume, but as western influences penetrated Japan, other beverages became popular. In 1965, consumption of beer surpassed the consumption of saké for the first time in Japan. Perhaps due to this threat of competition, or to a desire to return to tradition, the saké industry began to move toward more clear, user-friendly labels. There is now a general trend toward a better product, rather than a cheaper one, and a self-regulated labeling rule, established in 1975, has helped consumers know what they are buying. If non-rice adjuncts or flavoring are used, this is now listed on the label, as is information about ingredients, brewing methodology, and quality.

The word "saké" is a generic Japanese term for all alcoholic beverages. In 1973, the Central Brewers' Union began to use the term *nihonshu*, which merely means Japanese saké. (The character used as the suffix, *–shu*, refers to alcoholic beverages.) Legally, however, saké is known as *seishu,* loosely but ubiquitously rendered as refined saké. By law, *seishu* must be filtered through a mesh of some sort. Today, the term saké—plural as well as singular—suffices, and when differentiation is needed, *nihonshu* is brought into play. Rarely does one see the term *seishu* anywhere but on a label.

SAKÉ AND JAPANESE CULTURE

Historically, *nihonshu* has been closely tied to Japan's indigenous religion, Shinto. References to the relationship between saké and deities are found in the country's oldest histories, the *Kojiki* and *Nihon Shoki,* as well as in ancient myths known as *Jindaiki* and *Ame no Waka Hiko.*

Saké is used in religious ceremonies in all facets of Japanese life, particularly observances of a celebratory nature. The most common example can be observed at traditional Shinto wedding services, when a small glass of saké is exchanged between bride and groom. On New Year's Day, saké is ceremoniously tasted to celebrate the opening of another trip around the seasons. Before each of the six official Sumo wrestling tournaments held in Japan each year, the raised clay ring inside which the bouts take place is rebuilt, blessed, and dedicated by a Shinto priest, and saké (as well as rice) is buried in the center of the ring. This is an offering to gods within the earth for the safety of the competitors. Similarly, before new construction, a "groundbreaking" ceremony is performed, during which saké is placed in the ground as an offering for the safety and good fortune of the building.

The largest Tengu mask in Japan, located on the grounds of a shrine near Tentaka brewery in Tochigi Prefecture. Tengu are mischievous goblin-like creatures who are said to live in the mountains of Japan.

Shinto is a religion respecting many deities represented in nature. There are, in fact, ancient deities of saké brewing. The primary deity is a character called Matsuo-sama, who "resides" in a shrine at the foot of Mount Arashi in Kyoto. There are smaller shrines to Matsuo-sama all over the Japanese countryside. In fact, every *sakagura* in the country has a small in-house shrine (known as a *kami-dana*) to some deity, usually Matsuo-sama. Other such shrines are found near towns where head brewers, or *tōji*, reside, or where their labor organizations are located. Before heading off for the winter's work at various *kura*, they gather for a prayer, and likely a drink. At the start of each brewing season, owners and brewers gather with a Shinto clergyman in the *kura*, and pray before the *kami-dana* for a safe, successful season. This ceremony is as integral to the brewing season as the steaming of rice.

Another ceremony, *O-Miki*, is performed in a Shinto shrine with a priest. Shinto shrines contain a small tray with two curiously-shaped saké flasks, known as *Miki-dokkuri*, and a wide-mouthed saké cup, all of white porcelain. The saké in the flasks, also commonly referred to as *O-Miki*, is presented as a gift to the shrine. A small taste of saké is taken in a very ritualistic way, a sign of communion with godly powers, usually as an expression of petition for good fortune. It is believed that one takes a bit of the godforce into oneself by drinking a small taste of saké in this way.

Saké has always pervaded the ways of Japan, and will likely continue to do so. This alone will keep the saké world alive and healthy, regardless of how it needs to evolve in order to survive.

SAKÉ TODAY

The saké-brewing world has existed in its present form, more or less, for centuries. Along the way, some *kura* grew as enterprises to become very large, organized, powerful companies. Most, however, remained small companies, brewing a very small amount of saké in comparison to the large brewers.

However, things are changing. Few young people are willing to tolerate the harsh lifestyle of traditional brewing in the smaller breweries, where the work is seasonal and hard. Brewers are now turning to more local people and more realistic working hours, though the specialist *tōji* are still coming from afar.

The large breweries are immense, mass-production factories. They brew all year round in modern, temperature-controlled facilities. Most of the work is automated and on a mass-production scale. A large brewery may make as much saké in a single day as some of the smaller *kura* make in the course of their entire six-month brewing year. Here, too, the *tōji* system is intact, but there may be dozens of *kurabito* (brewery workers) under the *tōji* (head brewer). There are also sales teams and other business-related departments just to keep the whole operation running.

Many of the well-known big brewers are worthy of note for their consistently decent saké, but also for the stability they bring to the saké market in the form of well-established enterprises. Some of the largest names include Gekkeikan, Hakutsuru, Ozeki, Shochikubai, Kizakura, Kiku Masamune, Kenbishi, Sawanotsuru, Hakushika, and Shirayuki. A second tier of almost-as-large brewers might be represented by Sakura Masamune, Kamotsuru, Fukumasamune, Umenishiki, Fukumusume, Takashimizu, and Asahiyama. Many of the breweries have saké available in the United States which is either imported from Japan or brewed by local U.S. subsidiaries.

The consumption of saké in Japan is dropping, as it has been for many years. This is due to an increase in the consumption of beer and wine over the last several decades. However, the increase in both the production and consumption of premium saké is slowly but steadily increasing. Although it still accounts for less than twenty percent of the market in Japan, the heightened interest in saké brewing as a craft and in good saké in general is encouraging. Even so, good saké is now seeing stiff competition from wine, in particular imported red wine. The acknowledged health benefits and social appeal of wine have become well-established among consumers in Japan.

There are, at present, six saké breweries in the United States (all of which are introduced in Section Three). All were set up by Japanese brewing companies, and most are still operated by Japanese companies domiciled in Japan. Most are modern facilities that are quite sharp. The latest technology and modern equipment allows saké to be brewed in the United States with great efficiency, and although there are some Japanese employees present for guidance, most of the saké in the United States is brewed by Americans, for Americans.

The Craft of Making Saké

TYPES OF SAKÉ

Saké brewing, like any ancient craft, has its share of special terminology. Over the centuries, as new methods and products were introduced, new descriptive terms followed. Many of these terms are far from obvious in meaning, even to the Japanese. The Japanese-to-English translation barrier can cause further confusion.

Although learning the terminology is highly recommended in that it enhances the overall experience of drinking saké, one can certainly enjoy saké without knowing it. Most saké is fairly priced—in general, the price reflects the quality. Naturally, there are some overpriced saké (due to popularity and reputation, regardless of whether it is deserved), and there are some outstanding values as well. Usually, it will suffice to simply remember a name or a label. If you like what is inside, buy it again.

Most saké falls into one of nine related classifications. Three pieces of information are indicated by each of these classifications. The first is how far the rice was polished before brewing, which has a huge effect on quality and flavor profile. In general, the more a rice is milled, the higher the grade of saké. Although this practice can be taken too far, resulting in saké without much character, more highly polished rice usually leads to lighter, more complex flavor profiles. A second factor is how much handmade effort, care, and precision went into the brewing process. Although methods are not explicitly spelled out for each classification, the use of more labor-intensive brewing methods is implied with each increasing level. The third factor is whether or not distilled alcohol was added to the saké mash. This does not necessarily have a direct correlation to quality, at least not among premium grades of saké, but is rather a function of personal preference, as many people dislike the practice.

Here, then, are the basic definitions of the most commonly seen classifications of saké.

Futsuu-shu

This is "regular" saké that does not qualify for a special designation. Two-thirds of all saké falls into this category, including bland, tasteless, even bad-tasting products. This is not to say that all *futsuu-shu*—essentially a sort of default group—are bad. There are many enjoyable saké without a special designation, and it is important not to subject oneself to unnecessary prejudices based on the lack of such a special designation.

Honjōzō-shu and Junmai-shu

Both must be made with rice that has been milled to at least seventy percent, so that the outer thirty percent of the grains has been removed. *Junmai-shu* is made with nothing but rice, *kōji* (the mold that breaks starch into sugars), water, and yeast. It usually has a rich, full flavor, heavy and often a bit acidic. *Honjōzō-shu* is similar, but with a very small amount of alcohol added to the mash before pressing. This makes the saké a bit lighter, lower in acidity, and sometimes more fragrant.

Tokubetsu Honjōzō-shu and Tokubetsu Junmai-shu

These two terms are fairly commonly seen. *Tokubetsu* simply means "special," and these two types are essentially *junmai-shu* and *honjōzō-shu* that have been made in a *special* manner, indicating it is a notch or two above average. This special manner is supposed to be indicated on the label, but often it is not. Most often it refers to high quality rice, or above average polishing.

Ginjō-shu and *Junmai Ginjō-shu*

Saké of this grade is often lighter, more complex and delicate, and more fragrant than *junmai-shu* and *honjōzō-shu*. It is made with rice milled to at least sixty percent, but often much higher. Beyond this, in most cases every step of the complex brewing process is performed in old, time-consuming ways that provide a handmade touch of quality. The differences between regular *ginjō-shu* (sometimes called *honjōzō ginjō* for clarity, although this is not official terminology) and *junmai ginjō-shu* are similar to the differences between *honjōzō-shu* and *junmai-shu* described above. The small amount of alcohol added to *ginjō-shu* makes it lighter and more fragrant, whereas the *junmai ginjō-shu*, with no added alcohol, will likely be sturdier and often a touch more acidic. This distinction, too, is not always clear. Which is better is purely a matter of preference.

Daiginjō-shu and *Junmai Daiginjō-shu*

In both styles, *daiginjō-shu* represents the pinnacle of the brewer's craft. It is often made with the best saké rice, milled to at least fifty percent, although often the milling is taken as far as thirty-five percent (which means that sixty-five percent of the rice was ground away before brewing begins), and can be very fragrant, clean, delicate, and complex. Although there are many styles, and each varies with respect to these components, *daiginjō-shu* represents the culmination of the brewer's craft in each respective style.

As with the other two levels, regular *daiginjō-shu* (sometimes called *honjōzō daiginjō* for clarity, although this is not official terminology) can be lighter in body and more fragrant than *junmai daiginjō-shu*. This is not, however, a given, and whether or not alcohol has been added is not as relevant as the brewer's skill and intentions.

To merely describe the rice and flavor profile of this type of saké does not do justice to those who brewed it. It can be difficult, exhausting, and stressful to make. Although technology has helped immensely, split-second timing and constant human intervention based on intuition and experience are needed to respond to ever-changing conditions in the rice, water, and temperature. Brewing *daiginjō-shu* is truly an art and a craft of the highest level.

It is important to remember that the distinctions between various types of saké are often very subtle. There is a great deal of common ground between the classifications of saké. Many *junmai-shu,* for example, are fragrant and light, and could easily pass as *ginjō-shu,* as could some *honjōzō-shu.* There are also some slightly rough and gamy *ginjō-shu* that many would consider of a *junmai-shu* class. Except for obvious and extreme examples, most people could not identify the classification of a given saké in a blind tasting.

Understanding Saké Terms

Above and beyond the major classifications outlined above, here are a few other terms that go a long way in helping you determine what to expect from a given saké. These terms are not so much types or grades of saké as they are descriptions of how the saké has been handled or processed after brewing. Since such processes (or lack thereof) greatly affect the flavor profile, these terms appear on a saké's label if they apply.

Nama-zake
Nama-zake is simply saké that has not been pasturized. It is fresher, livelier, and more fragrant than pasteurized saké. People often comment that it tastes sweeter, although chemically there is no justification for this. Some connoisseurs feel that the special qualities of *nama-zake* overshadow other, more delicate aspects of the flavor. Others prize *nama-zake* precisely for its unique nuances. In the end, it is entirely a matter of personal preference. Whether or not a saké is *nama-zake* is unrelated to class, grade, or quality. There are both pasteurized and *nama-zake* versions of all grades of saké. Although all saké benefits from refrigerated storage, *nama-zake,* or unpasteurized saké, <u>must</u> be kept cold, or it will turn milky in color, and sweet-tart and yeasty in flavor and aroma, a condition called *hi-ochi.* (It won't hurt you, but it doesn't taste very good.)

Genshu
Genshu is undiluted saké, presented at its original strength of usually about twenty percent alcohol. Most

saké is cut with pure water to bring the alcohol level down to about sixteen percent, while *genshu* is not. The increased alcohol content can be overpowering for some, while others feel the added impact of the alcohol complements the brashness of a new brew. As with *nama-zake,* whether or not a saké is *genshu* is unrelated to its class or grade.

Nigori-zake

Nigori-zake means cloudy saké, and is saké that has a good amount of the fermenting mash left inside. This is done either by pressing (to separate the saké and lees) with a very coarse mesh that allows much of the semi-solids to pass through, or by adding some of the lees back into the saké after pressing. By legal definition, saké must be pressed by passing it through a mesh. In order to conform with this law, one of the above two methods is used to create this creamy, rich type of saké.

There is a whole range of flavor profiles for *nigori-zake,* some being quite sweet while others can be tart and acidic. While tasty and fun, *nigori-zake* does not generally offer the same potential for gourmet appreciation as most types of premium saké.

Funa-shibori

Most saké is pressed by machine. *Funa-shibori* is pressed from the lees in the old manner, by filling meter-long canvas bags with *moromi,* laying them in a large wooden box or *fune,* and cranking down the lid to squeeze out the liquid. It usually yields a more distinctive saké.

Shizuku

Extravagant and wonderful, this is saké that was separated from the lees by allowing the saké to drip out from the bags, with no pressure applied.

Tōbin-gakoi

This term indicates that a saké was separated into eighteen-liter bottles (*tōbin*) upon pressing, and usually that it was produced by *funa-shibori* or *shizuku* methods. Since the saké is separated into these bottles, there will of course be extremely subtle differences between each eighteen-liter bottle. This allows the brewer to choose the absolute best part of a batch to, for example, submit to a tasting competition. It is rarely seen outside Japan.

Ko-shu

Aging saké is fairly rare, and saké brewers have only been actively experimenting with aging saké for about the last thirty years. Aged saké, or *ko-shu*, is heavier, with denser, sometimes danker flavors. Whether or not a saké has been aged is unrelated to the grade, for saké of any quality can be aged and called *ko-shu*. (More is said about aging saké on pages 32–34.)

Nama-chozō

Whereas most saké is pasteurized twice, *nama-chozō* is stored for about six months, then pasteurized once before shipping. Also known as *nama-tsume*, the difference between *nama-chozō* and fully pasteurized saké is not always obvious.

Clockwise, from top left: Kurabito *hanging bags of* moromi, *allowing the just-brewed saké to drip out—this method of pressing is known as* shizuku; *saké being pressed into 18-liter bottles called* tōbin; *freshly pressed sake in* tōbin.

Hiya-oroshi

Like *nama-chozō,* this saké is pasteurized once before the fall release, but before the six-month storage period instead of after it. Again, there is not usually a pronounced difference between *hiya-oroshi* and fully pasteurized saké.

Yamahai Shikomi and *Kimoto*

These are centuries-old, labor-intensive techniques for creating the *moto* yeast starter mash. Saké made with these processes tends to be a bit stronger and gamier, with more pronounced—but still subtle—bitter, acidic, and sweet flavors. As the methods are difficult and time-consuming, they are rarely used in saké produced in the United States, though they are fairly common in Japan.

Shiboritate

A bit brasher and younger than most saké, this has been very recently brewed and pressed, then bottled without the customary six-month maturation period.

THE COMPONENTS OF SAKÉ

Rice

Rice holds a unique significance in Japan. It has more meaning in Japanese culture than simply being the national staple food. Long ago, taxes and even samurai stipends were paid in units of rice called *koku.* One *koku* is roughly the amount of rice needed to feed one person for a year. Because saké is brewed from rice, it is often used in cultural and religious ceremonies, much like wine is used in cultural and religious ceremonies in the West. When comparing saké to wine, as is often done, it is only natural to compare rice to grapes. Many Westerners, through their love of wine, are knowledgeable about how soil and weather affect the grapes, and in turn the wine made from them.

Growing rice is an equally deep and complex function of soil, weather, and skill. Grape-oriented reasoning would lead one to think that if the rice is good, it should be usable as is, without milling away the outside portion. To use unmilled whole rice grains would be like throwing in the vines and leaves with the grapes, or leaving the grape skins in through the entire fermentation process. In both cases, components are left out because they will not ferment.

Grapes, for the most part, ferment themselves, and while yeast purity, appropriate temperature, and sanitation must be maintained, the grapes make the wine. Saké, on the other hand, is deliberately and carefully crafted each step of the way. Rice is only the beginning. Saké must be supervised and coaxed, instructed and pampered. If left alone, it could go down any one of a thousand paths. A well-brewed saké is a unique expression of the interplay between the soil, weather, and farming skill, as well as the intentions, experience, and intuition of the brewer.

This is one reason why there are no "vintage" years in saké, as there are in wine. To be sure, there are good and bad years for rice. But a less than optimum batch can be improved with extra effort by the *tōji* (head brewer) at the *kura*. Also, just because a *kura* used proper saké rice does not guarantee a good product, just as wonderful saké has been brewed with less than sterling rice. In truth, most saké (i.e. average, mass-produced saké) is not brewed with good saké rice, but with less expensive table rice. Much of this saké is very drinkable, in the same way that much table wine throughout the world is perfectly drinkable. But in general, decent saké rice leads to decent saké, and premium saké is indeed brewed from good saké rice.

There are dozens of varieties of saké rice, known as *shuzō kōtekimai*, or *kōtekimai* for short, and simply called *sakamai* in the everyday language of the *kura*. In Japan, saké rice is an official classification given by the government to varieties that qualify on the basis of several parameters, such as size and weight of the grains. However, saké is not classified by the rice from which it was brewed. Rarely, if ever, is the name of the rice variety considered to define the type of saké.

Growing *sakamai* is a delicate and precarious endeavor. The plant is top-heavy and awkward, vulnerable to severe damage by storms and typhoons. This type of rice almost systematically resists attempts at mass production. It doesn't respond well to strong insecticides and fertilizers, and requires more water and attention than regular rice.

Soil quality and weather are even more important than for regular rice. Things are further complicated by the fact that what saké rice farmers aim for is a plant that is held a bit below its full potential. Just as the best grapes come from rough and scrawny vines that seem to be barely surviving, the best saké rice comes from stalks that are kept a bit underfed and hungry, clinging to life with little fanfare or glory. It is a difficult balance to strike.

Sakamai stalks are significantly taller, and the grains larger, than those of table rice. Grain size is important because it allows the rice to be polished and otherwise processed in a way that maximizes the yield and finer qualities of the rice. *Sakamai* generally has what is known as a *shinpaku,* or "white heart." *Shinpaku* refers to the opaque white center of the rice grain. As the rice kernel develops starch while growing, it is stored in the center of the grain. This causes minuscule air pockets to develop between cells, diffusing light and creating the opaque whiteness. *Shinpaku* indicates a high ratio of starch to proteins and fats, and an easy-to-process distribution of them within the grain. The higher the ratio of grains with *shinpaku,* the better a batch of rice will absorb water and the more easily the *kōji* can work its way into the center of the rice kernels. Good *sakamai* will have a visible *shinpaku* in about eighty percent of the polished grains.

All prefectures grow some *sakamai,* with the exception of Hokkaido, Tokyo, Kagoshima (the only prefecture where saké is not brewed), and Okinawa. The best *sakamai,* however, grow best in particular regions. In fact, areas within prefectures are often given a designation indicating the quality of the rice grown there, such as "Special A" or "Special B." These are relatively important, but by no means absolute, indicators of rice quality.

Almost all modern saké rice is the result of crossbreeding. (Two notable exceptions are Omachi and Kame no O.) New varieties of *sakamai* are being developed all the time, in an effort to produce shorter stalks, easier harvesting with machinery, and higher yields. A great amount of prize-winning saké is brewed from a rice known as Yamada Nishiki—a name to remember. But there is much overlap between saké made with one rice and that made from another.

Water

Long ago, *kura* were often set up in a particular place because of its water quality. In fact, the largest brewing region in Japan, the Nada ward in Kobe, exists because of the famous water found there. The water of the region has been nicknamed Miyamizu because of its superior saké brewing qualities. As with rice, today water can be enhanced to some degree, to produce precisely what is required for brewing. However, most *kura* use pure, original water sources with little or no filtering.

Most water used for saké in Japan is either well water, often from deep wells, or water from underground rivers created from melted snow runoff from the mountains that has seeped through layers of rock. The major saké styles came into being based on whether the local water was hard, soft, or somewhere in between, with various mineral and chemical components affecting flavor, impact, viscosity, and mouth feel. Water, in fact, may have more of a profound effect on the final product than any other factor.

Kōji

This mold, technically called *Aspergillus Oryzae,* is so crucial to the brewing process that it could be the subject of several chapters, if not entire books. Note that *kōji* refers to the finished product, whereas the mold spores before being propagated onto rice is known as *kōji-kin,* or *tane-kōji. Kōji-kin,* in the form of a dark, fine powder, is sprinkled on steamed rice that has been cooled. The rice is then taken to a special room within the kura maintained at a higher than average humidity and temperature. Over the next thirty-six to fifty hours, the developing *kōji* is checked and mixed constantly. The final product looks like rice grains with a slight frosting on them, and smells faintly of sweet chestnuts. *Kōji* is used at least four times throughout the saké brewing process, and is always made fresh and used immediately.

The slightest differences in *kōji* can affect the flavor of the final product. As the traditional process for making it is so labor-intensive, many changes have come about. Some breweries now use large machines for part or all of the process, attempting to imitate the skill and intuition of the human masters. Others use walls paneled in stainless steel rather than wood. It is interesting to note, however, that almost all super premium saké like *daiginjō-shu* is brewed with handmade *kōji*.

Yeast

The choice of yeast in saké brewing is extremely important, and will affect the basic nature of the saké. Most noticeably fragrance, but also flavor aspects such as acidity, are intimately connected to the yeast and its successful propagation.

Yeast converts sugar to alcohol and carbon dioxide. It is the heart of the creation of all alcoholic beverages. There are innumerable strains of yeast, and those used in making bread, beer, and wine are different from those used for saké. As fermentation proceeds, different yeast strains produce esters, various acids, and other chemical compounds in different quantities, all of which affect the nuances of fragrance and flavor. The compounds produced are also dependent on the temperature at which fermentation takes place.

There are currently dozens of strains of yeast in use, each with a specific special quality. New strains are isolated in saké brewing research centers all the time. A particular yeast strain may have a strong affinity with a given rice variety or water of a region. The choice of yeast is based on these factors, combined with the style of saké the brewer wishes to create.

In the early 1900s, the Central Brewers Union first made available pure, isolated yeast strains (usually from particularly good tanks of saké from larger breweries) to *kura* across the nation, in small glass vials. These yeast strains have since been assigned numbers by the Central Brewers Union. Since this practice began, fifteen strains have been available, although not all are still in use. Yeasts #7, #9, and #10 are perhaps the most important at present. Yeast #7 is the single most commonly used yeast in the country, with its mellow fragrance and robust strength during fermentation. Yeast #9 is the most common yeast for *ginjō-shu*, due to its wonderful fragrance-creating abilities, and fairly healthy constitution during fermentation. Yeast #10 produces a lower-acid, fine-grained flavor in saké, but is a bit fickle at all but the lowest fermentation temperatures.

In addition to the publicly available yeast strains, many others are used on a smaller scale. Many of these are proprietary, having been developed by *kura* and used only in-house, or, more commonly, developed by prefectural brewing research institutes and used only by *kura* in that prefecture.

Often the yeast used is listed on the label. However, as more and more yeast strains come into use, it becomes cumbersome to try and remember them. It is certainly enough to simply be aware that various yeast strains exist, and to learn their names and characteristics over time.

OTHER INFLUENCES ON SAKÉ

Rice Milling (Seimai-buai)

Within a grain of saké rice, the fermentable starches are located in the center, surrounded by proteins and fats and other components that can affect the flow

Clockwise, from top left: Kurabito *mixing* kōji *to keep the temperature distribution even and ensure smooth propagation of the mold;* kōji *being put into* kōji-buta, *small trays that help the* kōji *develop evenly and thoroughly; stacks of* kōji-buta, *small trays for preparing hand-made* kōji.

of fermentation and lead to off-flavors. The more rice is milled, the more undesirable components are removed. The difference is easily apparent. Flavor, fragrance, and mouth feel are all greatly affected. Tasting a saké brewed with less than highly polished rice, especially after sipping a *daiginjō-shu* made with very highly polished rice, can leave an impression of roughness and a grainy aftertaste. This is not always unpleasant, and often adds character, but there is a noticeable difference.

In Japanese, the degree of milling is called the *seimai-buai.* It refers to the percentage of the original size of the grains that remains after milling. Thus, rice with a *seimai-buai* of sixty percent has had the outer forty percent "polished" away, ground into white powder. This powder has various uses in cooking and in traditional confectioneries, but it is not used in the saké brewing process (although some large brewing companies use it to make cheap saké).

The minimum *seimai-buai* for *ginjō-shu* is sixty percent, and the minimum for the subclass *daiginjō-shu* is fifty percent, but very often much more is removed. Although it is strictly a matter of personal taste, it is possible to take milling too far. If the rice is polished too highly, the resulting saké can be tasteless and uninteresting, regardless of how clean the flavor might be.

The Adding of Distilled Alcohol

All saké that does not have the word *"junmai"* on its label somewhere contains pure distilled alcohol, which is added to the fermenting mash, or *moromi,* near the end of the fermentation period. The addition of distilled alcohol to fermenting saké is a centuries-old practice, appearing in brewing texts as far back as the 1600s, although it was not necessarily widely practiced. Liquor laws established for tax purposes in the Meiji Era of the late nineteenth century state that saké is a beverage brewed from rice, water, and *kōji-kin.* There is no mention of added alcohol, and therefore the process was banned officially. Thus, hold some purists, anything other than *junmai-shu* is not really saké. However, the addition of distilled alcohol was again legalized during World War II to make up for rice shortages, and it is still legal today, creating a chink in the purist armor. The question of what is historically "real saké" may depend on who is considered the authority—the government or the saké-brewing craftspeople.

Centuries ago, alcohol was sometimes added (in the form of a distilled beverage called *shōchū*) to enliven fragrance and bolster flavor. Until the early twentieth century, rice polishing was fairly crude and inefficient, and this was evidenced in the flavor of saké. As technology improved the process, it became less necessary to add anything, and the practice all but died. During the war, brewers improvised, using copious amounts of ethyl alcohol distilled from corn and other grains. Flavorings and chemicals were added to create a palatable potion at great cost reduction, and with significantly less rice.

Although rice stocks were replenished after the war, the practice had become more or less universal. It was not until the late 1960s that anyone began brewing *junmai-shu* again. Eventually, a movement started to return to original brewing practices, spurred by discerning consumers and conscientious brewers. Even so, at present, most Japanese saké does contain added alcohol, for purely economic reasons. Only about twelve percent of all saké produced in Japan is *junmai-shu*.

Within the realm of premium saké, the addition of alcohol serves several very real purposes, most notably that of enhancing fragrance. Adding alcohol also lightens the flavor a bit, often lowering the overall acidity. Purists believe that rice polishing technology and sanitation have risen to the level where adding alcohol should not be necessary. In the end, it is hardly a raging battle. There are *kura* that brew only *junmai-shu,* and certain saké pubs and retailers that sell nothing else, but most people drink what they like, not limiting themselves to one realm or the other.

In the United States, however, things are different. The addition of any distilled alcohol qualifies the entire beverage as distilled, and creating it is illegal with only a brewing license (as opposed to a distilling license). All saké produced in the United States is therefore *junmai-shu, junmai ginjō-shu*, or *junmai daiginjō-shu*. Although it is legal to import non-*junmai* saké from Japan, it is taxed at distilled spirit rates and is not common. It is therefore unlikely that the discussion of which is better will amount to much in the United States.

Aging

Almost all saké is aged to some degree. Just-brewed saké *(shibori-tate)* can have a fresh, crisp, lively appeal, but the flavors may be in competition with each other, and need mellowing. Therefore, most saké, traditionally brewed in winter and early spring, is aged over the summer and released in the fall. The length of this aging period varies from brewer to brewer. Six months is standard, but some *kura* age their saké for a year or two before releasing it. Naturally, they are deliberately aiming for a certain result, usually a more balanced flavor.

Most saké is not intended to be aged any longer after it is shipped, but is rather to be consumed within about six months after shipment. This is not to say that saké will *necessarily* go bad if it gets too old; there are no hard or fast rules. However, the potential for a saké changing significantly over time is great; there is

A sugidama (left), a tightly bound ball of Japanese cedar leaves, is a traditional symbol of Japanese saké and saké breweries. Made each year in the fall and hung in front of all Japanese saké breweries, the green leaves slowly turn to brown as the seasons change. It is said that the brewery's saké has aged an appropriate amount of time and is ready for drinking when the color transformation is complete.

a good chance it will become cloying and unbalanced, with sour, bitter, and musty flavors being drawn out. Consider this to be the rule of thumb: in order to taste a saké *just as the brewer intended you to taste it,* consume it within six months or so, and keep it stored in a cool, dark place. (Refrigeration is best.) Note, too, that for these reasons and others, the concept of a "vintage year" does not really exist.

Aged saké is generally referred to as *ko-shu.* However, this catch-all phrase can also refer to inadvertently aged saké, saké not sold fast enough or left to lay around a *kura* or home. As such, many *kura* now market their aged saké under the term *chōki jukusei-shu* (long-term matured saké).

Long ago, almost no saké was aged beyond the customary six months or so. At warm temperatures, saké can change drastically, and as there was no refrigeration in centuries past, it was difficult to ensure saké stayed drinkable for long periods of time. Rice milling technology and brewing techniques were not as advanced as they are today, and saké flavors soon went awry with age. Beyond these technical reasons, there were economical concerns as well. Until just before World War II, saké brewers were taxed on the saké that they brewed, not only on what they sold. Naturally, brewers wanted to sell all their saké as quickly as possible because they had already paid taxes on it. Because of this, pre-World War II Japan was not an environment that encouraged experimentation in the aging arena.

However, given the popularity of aging in other fine sipping beverages, as well as changes in the taxation laws, brewers have been experimenting over the past thirty years to learn more about the possibility of further aging saké.

There is a lot of variation in aging techniques. Many *kura* age their saké at low temperatures, sometimes even at freezing temperatures. This slows changes, making it easier to control the results of the aging process. Other *kura* age their saké at room temperature, causing more prominent changes in flavor and color. Some breweries use a combination of temperatures, with varied results.

There are also variations in aging vessels. Until the late 1800s, cedar tanks were used in brewing. Naturally, the wood's flavor and smell were prominent, especially if the saké sat a long time. Today, ceramic-lined and stainless steel tanks are used, and sometimes saké is aged in these tanks. This allows sediment to drop out over time, so the saké can be removed and put into bottles, leaving the dregs behind. Some saké is transferred to bottles soon after brewing and aged there from the beginning.

When it is good, *ko-shu* has a wide array of flavors. Generally soft and mellow, it can have a solid, earthy presence underlined with bitter tones and good acidity. Some are fragrant, some quiet, but most are rich and chewy. Quite a lot of *ko-shu* is wonderful slightly warmed, perhaps more so than other types of saké, yet some is much better slightly chilled. *Ko-shu* is certainly not to everyone's taste, and it is also generally a bit more expensive than other saké. It is still, after decades, in its experimental stages.

Region

The entire land mass of Japan would fit inside the state of California, yet the diversity of culture, language, and cuisine is astounding. Accordingly, saké from different regions of Japan have distinct representative styles, shaped by a number of factors. Some of these factors are comparable to conditions in the world of wine, while others, less obvious, are unique to Japan.

Rice has been a major influencing factor in the development of regional styles and distinctions. Long ago, only locally grown rice was used, and this would impart its special characteristics on the final product. Although these styles are, for the most part, long-established, today rice is less of a factor, since there are no limitations on keeping rice in the region where it was grown. Although locally grown rice is still used most often, some of the best saké rice from western Japan is routinely shipped all over the country (albeit in small quantities).

Saké flavor profiles are further affected by local cuisine. People living near the coasts and in large populous plains had access to fresh fish and other foods with relatively light flavors. Those living in mountainous or otherwise isolated areas had to rely on preserved foods, often fermented, with stronger flavors. Naturally, local saké is brewed to complement the indigenous food.

A third factor which influences the flavor of saké is the culture surrounding saké brewing. Brewery workers were rarely, if ever, the owners of the *kura.* (Indeed, even today there are few examples of this.) They were seasonal employees, farmers from the countryside who were idle in the winter. The head brewer of each team, known as a *tōji,* often resided near other *tōji* when at home in the summer, as most of these seasonal workers came from the same towns. (This practice is still common today.) They formed groups similar to labor unions, and exchanged techniques and notes, creating brewing styles based on certain methodologies. *Tōji* groups from different areas performed the various steps in distinct ways, which led to identifiable differences in their respective saké, traits and tendencies that are still evident in saké styles today. Often the *ryūha,* or regional group from which a *tōji* has come, is listed on the back label of a saké bottle.

Due to the modern distribution system and transportation infrastructure, regional distinctions are not nearly as clear as they once were. The same wonderful technology that allows one to get saké from anywhere with relative ease also transforms the local market of any *kura* into a national market. Competition comes streaming in, as does marketing information and public opinion. The tastes of the masses change. Trends are, to some degree, homogenizing. Whether they like it or not, many brewers feel they need to make saké that is popular.

Still, enough regional distinction remains to keep things interesting. In fact, many brewers go out of their way to maintain traditional flavor profiles. Knowing the region or prefecture where a saké was brewed is an important aspect of connoisseurship in Japan. Here's a look at the top saké brewing regions in Japan, and their representative styles.

The Nada district of Kobe, Hyogo Prefecture

Approximately one-third of all saké produced in Japan comes from this short strip of land near the port of Kobe. It is responsible for more advances in brewing technology, market expansion, and quality than any other locale. Kobe's seaside location facilitated the shipping of saké to Edo, or Tokyo, the capital, to quench the thirst of the hedonistic upper class. Subsequently, countless breweries flourished here. Many are giants that dominate the industry today. In fact, nine of Japan's top thirteen brewers (in terms of volume) are located in the Nada district. There are more than fifty tiny *kura* there as well. The region has been decimated several times, including bombing during World War II and the Great Hanshin Earthquake of 1995, which put ten percent of the smaller breweries out of business.

One of the country's finest saké rice, a variety known as Yamada Nishiki, grows well here. In the mid-nineteenth century, a water source called Miyamizu, which flows down from nearby Mt. Rokko and is filtered beneath the earth, was empirically determined to be perfect for making premium saké.

Hyogo saké is usually dry and mellow. Generally, the fragrance is rarely prominent, rather demure and self-effacing. The flavor is settled and full, with lots of subtleties. It is definitely not flowery or fruity in style. The region's hard water lends a crispness and solidity. Kobe saké is often referred to as *danseiteki,* or masculine.

The Fushimi Ward of Kyoto, Kyoto Prefecture

Less than an hour by train from Kobe lies Kyoto, Japan's ancient capital. Its Fushimi region is home to more than half of Kyoto's approximately seventy *kura,* and in many ways is a complement to the Nada region of Kyoto. Together they firmly establish the Kansai area of western Japan as the country's predominant saké-brewing region.

Much of the saké brewed in Kyoto was for the Imperial court and its nobles, a market that demanded the best. By the end of the thirteenth century there were three hundred breweries here. Competition fostered progress. Many significant technical developments, such as the isolation of *kōji* spores and the use of a yeast starter, took place then.

Still, Kyoto did not begin producing saké on a large scale until the late 1800s, and could not compete in the Edo market due to the lack of a seaport. However, the development of a rail system changed all that, and Kyoto soon became second in production, which is where it stands today. In fact, Kyoto makes thirteen percent of Japan's saké. Gekkeikan, the country's largest brewer, is here, as are two more in the top seven. The region has its share of smaller *kura* as well.

Kyoto saké is soft, spreading well across the palate and melting in quietly. With very delicate undercurrents that are often intuitively sensed rather than overtly tasted, it is often described as feminine, especially when compared with saké from Nada. Rich yet unpretentious, good Kyoto saké can render you speechless with its nobility and grace.

Niigata Prefecture

In the 1970s, saké from smaller brewers in the countryside became popular as a more exclusive alternative to the nationally-distributed brands available everywhere. These country saké came to be known as *jizake,* loosely translated as "local saké." "Micro-brewed" might be a more appropriate term, although that term, too, has its limitations.

The image of *jizake* is that of uniqueness and character, and Niigata quickly became the most popular source for saké bearing this image. The *tōji* of this region use highly polished rice and exacting filtering techniques to create an inimitable style. They are aided by the cold climate and relative isolation by mountains, as well as good regional rice and pure mountain water. In the minds of many, it's simply the best, and people who don't know a lot about saké will buy something famous from Niigata "to be safe." The prefecture is third in terms of production, behind Hyogo and Kyoto, and production has increased significantly over the past twenty years. It is home to just over one hundred *kura.*

Niigata saké is clean and refined, and perhaps too commonly is used by some people as a yardstick for all saké. The flavor is referred to as *tanrei-karakuchi,* or light and dry. Typically, it disappears from your palate very quickly. For the record, many people also find its taste a bit too clean and smooth, and not terribly interesting. Yet, many first-time saké drinkers will choose it in a blind tasting as their favorite.

Akita Prefecture

The Tohoku region in northern Japan is home to Akita prefecture, one of the most important saké-brewing regions of the last hundred years. Although it may not enjoy the history or esteem of some other areas, the saké from Akita, the fourth largest producing area in Japan, is among the best. Blessed with nice, cold winters and fast flowing water, the quality of the prefecture's brew has been sterling since the beginning of this century. Its slogan is *"Bishu Ōkoku,"* or "the empire of beautiful saké."

In the late 1800s, when it became easy to get a brewing license, many *kura* were established in the region, where they found thirsty customers among the local coal and silver miners. There are about fifty *kura* in Akita, and their presence is always noted in the new saké tasting competitions held each spring. Over the last ten years, Akita brewers have perfected the use of a yeast strain isolated in the prefectural saké research institute called AK-1 (A is for Akita, K is for *kōbo,* or yeast). AK-1 tends to produce very fragrant saké and is well suited to traditional Akita styles. However, it calls for fermenting at lower temperatures for longer periods of time. Recently it has become available to brewers nationwide under a different name.

Akita saké is rich and well-rounded, yet soft, with a layered, detailed construction. It is generally neutral rather than overtly dry. Lower grade, regular saké from Akita tends to exhibit more of these qualities, while the premium *ginjō-shu* is often much more fragrant and complex.

Hiroshima Prefecture

Saké production has flourished in Hiroshima since the Heian Era (794–1192), when it was supported by local feudal lords. The product is quite distinct, due to the area's relatively soft water. Originally, this soft water proved problematic, since local brewers were using methods that had worked well in places like Nada, whose water was significantly harder.

Then along came Senzaburo Miura in the late 1800s. Miura studied brewing in Kyoto, where the water was almost as soft as Hiroshima's. Upon returning to Hiroshima, he shared his technique with the local brewers; it involved using *kōji* that was in more advanced stages, to make up for the lackadaisical yeast activity.

The brewers applied his lessons well. From the 1960s through the 1980s, Hiroshima saké won more gold and silver awards in the national tax department new-saké tasting competitions than that of any other prefecture. On the strength of the city's Saijō region, Hiroshima is fifth or sixth in terms of national production, depending on the year.

Hiroshima saké is fairly easy to recognize. The fragrance is generally pronounced, and the flavor spreads fully around the palate. It is softer, and usually sweeter, than most saké. The softer water helps it melt into your tongue, making it easier to discern subtleties, of which there are many. It is clean, with any number of undertones.

Fukushima Prefecture

Cold and snowy, Fukushima's northern winters are perfect for saké brewing. Taking advantage of these conditions are eighty or so *kura* of all sizes. Some produce only fifty kiloliters a year; how they survive is a mystery. Others brew perhaps one thousand times that. Yet quality standards are relatively high, as is consistency. About seventy percent of the saké in Fukushima, which is adjacent to Niigata in the Tohoku region, comes from Aizu-Wakamatsu city and closely neighboring Kitakata city. An added attraction for visitors to the area is the attractive architectural style of the *kura* buildings. Ancient, white-plaster buildings are everywhere, but fading fast as neither the materials nor the craftsmen exist to maintain them.

Several years ago, in an attempt to produce more premium *ginjō-shu,* the prefectural saké research institute here isolated a yeast called F1-07, selected to improve the local product. The result is a lighter, crisper saké, significantly more fragrant than most Fukushima saké, with a bit less of an acid presence. Almost every *kura* in the prefecture uses it to some degree.

Fukushima saké is slightly sweet to slightly dry, excessive in neither direction. It is generally soft on the palate, with minimal fragrance. It tends to be light in body, but with a hidden something that makes you want to come back for more (a quality called *umami* in Japanese). It is definitely saké one can drink a lot of, by itself or with food.

Other Regions

There are forty-seven prefectures in Japan, and all but one brew at least some saké. Not every prefecture produces saké of unique character or great volume, but some do make saké that is unique and wonderful. Although they may not brew in volume comparable to the above six, they are significant for their distinction of style. Here are a few of those regions, and the history and reasons behind their great saké.

Shizuoka Prefecture

Famous as the source of Japan's best green tea, Shizuoka is located on the Tōkaido, the historic road between Edo (present-day Tokyo) and the Kyoto-Osaka-Kobe region. Proximity to this mighty highway has helped Shizuoka saké spread both east and west. Although it never has been one of the area's major products, clean rivers filling deep wells and melted snow running down from nearby Mt. Fuji provide the water for plenty of good saké.

Due to the efforts of the prefecture's industrial technology center, Shizuoka saké emerged in 1985 to shine in national saké tastings. The area was also instrumental in the discovery of several new pure yeast strains.

Light and fragrant, with a lower than usual acidity, Shizuoka produces saké one can drink a lot of without getting bored or finding it cloying. It is generally only slightly on the dry side, often laced with a gentle fruitiness. As there are only thirty-five *kura* in the prefecture, none of them very large, Shizuoka saké can be a bit difficult to find, but it is well worth the search.

Kochi Prefecture

Modern-day Kochi prefecture was once known as the Tosa region. Tosa played an active part in the Meiji Restoration, but more relevantly, it has long been famous for its drinkers. Warriors, politicians, and writers from Tosa were all famous for imbibing massive amounts of saké. Apparently, the tradition continues today.

There are only twenty or so *kura* in this prefecture on the small island of Shikoku. The weather is relatively warm, which means that, until the recent advent of refrigeration and water-filled cooling jackets, standard brewing methods had to be adjusted. Still, Kochi saké has a recognizable style, owing not so much to the water or rice of the region, but rather to the fact that everyone drank so much. It is made to be easy to drink in quantity, and it is.

Kochi saké is actually the driest in the entire country. Although Niigata saké is dry, crisp, and complex, Kochi's is more approachable. It is soft and smooth as water, but it opens in flavor as it makes its way in. Its fragrance is generally subdued. Acidity can often be high, so it goes well with slightly oily fish. The *umami,* that satisfying, elusive presence, fills the palate afterward. It is said that Kochi saké was formulated to not cause hangovers, even if more than one's share is consumed.

Yamagata Prefecture

Tucked near the northwest corner of Japan's main island, Honshu, Yamagata is surrounded by mountains on three sides, with a stretch open to the Japan Sea. Lacking a port of any significance, and given its out-of-the-way location, distribution was not Yamagata's forte. Its saké developed in relative isolation, and never received the attention it deserves. Only a third of the product brewed by the fifty *kura* leaves the prefecture. The hometown people clearly prefer their local brew, which constitutes ninety percent of all saké consumed there.

Yamagata saké is relatively full in body, but clean, often with a good, sturdy acid presence. It seems to have an abundance of personal character, uniquely, yet almost magically, balanced.

Like many other prefectures, Yamagata has put a lot of effort into yeast and rice development. For several years, local *kura* have used a variety of rice called Dewa 33, which in Japanese is a pun referring to the old name of the region and the surrounding mountains.

THE SAKÉ BREWING PROCESS

The process of brewing saké is easily the most complex of any beverage on earth. Although it has continually undergone technical refinements over the last several hundred years, the basic procedure has remained the same.

Saké is brewed, as opposed to simply being fermented (like wine) or distilled (like vodka or whiskey). Its process is similar to beer in that both begin with a grain containing starches. As with beer, those starches must be broken down into sugars before yeast can be added and fermentation can begin. Unlike beer, however, saké's primary grain lacks the potential to produce enzymes, as its husks have been milled away.

Enter the mighty *kōji* mold, an enzyme-producing mold which is very carefully and precisely propagated onto steamed rice. As this mold works its way into the steamed grains, the enzymes produced in the process break down the starches into fermentable sugars. Yeast is then introduced, and fermentation takes place in an open vat.

One big difference between saké and beer is that the *kōji* and yeast are working together in the same fermentation tank. In other words, saccharification and fermentation take place simultaneously, not sequentially as they do in beer. This aspect of the process is unique to saké production.

The many steps of the actual brewing process are very closely interrelated. Each step affects everything else on down the line, so that each step is extremely important. The general flow is described below.

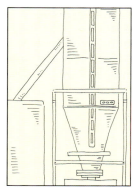

Rice polishing machine

Washing rice

■ First, the rice is milled, or "polished." This must be done gently to avoid cracking the kernels or generating too much heat, which adversely affects water absorption. *Nuka,* the white powder left after polishing, is washed away. The rice is then soaked to attain a certain water content deemed optimum for steaming that particular rice, which is an extremely important parameter. The more a rice has been polished, the faster it absorbs water and the shorter the soaking time. Often, it is soaked for as little as a stopwatch-measured minute, but sometimes—for less expensive saké—it remains immersed overnight.

One of the most important advances in the saké brewing process is the improvement in rice-polishing equipment. Originally, rice was stomped in a vat to remove the husks. Later, water wheels and grinding stones were used. Today, computer-controlled machines polish off the specified percentage of the grain in a specified amount of time—the more slowly it is polished, the better.

Koshiki (*rice steamer*)

■ Steam is introduced through the bottom of the steaming vat (traditionally called a *koshiki*) to work its way through the rice. This process produces rice of a firmer consistency, with a slightly harder outside surface, and softer center. Generally, a batch of steamed rice is divided, with some set aside to have *kōji* mold sprinkled over it, and some going directly to the fermentation vat.

Making kōji

■ In a special room maintained at a higher temperature and humidity, the rice sprinkled with *kōji* is laid out and monitored as often as every two hours in order to maintain the proper temperature. After thirty-six to fifty hours, the completed *kōji* looks a bit like rice with a white frosting, and smells faintly like sweet chestnuts. *Kōji* production is, in a sense, the heart of the entire brewing process.

■ A yeast starter (*shubō* or *moto*) is created by mixing finished *kōji*, plain steamed white rice, water, and pure yeast cells. Over the next two weeks, a mixture with a very high concentration of yeast cells—up to 100 million in one teaspoon—is developed.

■ After the mixture is moved to a larger tank, more rice, *kōji*, and water are added in three successive stages over four days, roughly doubling the size of the batch each

Fermentation tanks

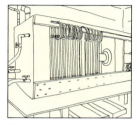

Saké pressing machine

Shizuku *method of pressing*

time. This is the main mash, or *moromi,* and as it ferments over the following eighteen to thirty-two days, its temperature and other parameters (like *nihonshu-do* and acidity) are measured and adjusted to precisely create the flavor profile being sought.

■ When everything is just right (no easy decision!), the saké is pressed, in a process called *jōsō.* Through one of several methods, the white lees *(kasu)* and unfermented solids are pressed away, and the clear saké runs off. Today, most saké is pressed with a huge, accordion-like machine that squeezes the *moromi* between balloon-like inflating panels, making disposal of the *kasu* simple. Much premium saké, however, is still pressed in the old, traditional method, in which the *moromi* is put into long canvas bags, laid in a wooden box, and squeezed out by cranking the lid into the box. In the extravagant *shizuku* method, the saké is permitted to drip out of the bags, with no pressure applied.

■ After sitting for a few days to let even more solids settle out, the saké is usually charcoal filtered to adjust flavor and color. This filtration process *(rōka)* is done to different degrees at different breweries, and determines much about the final flavor profile.

Most saké is then pasteurized: it is heated quickly as it passes through a pipe immersed in hot water. This process kills bacteria and deactivates enzymes that would likely affect flavor and color later on. Saké that is not pasteurized, called *nama-zake,* maintains a certain freshness of flavor, but it must be kept refrigerated.

Saké aging in tanks

■ Finally, most saké is aged about six months, rounding out the flavor, before it is shipped. Before shipping, it is usually pasteurized one more time, and tanks of saké of the same grade are blended to ensure consistency. Water is also added to reduce the naturally occurring alcohol content from approximately twenty percent to about sixteen percent.

The Art of Appreciating Saké

Until you have had the opportunity to taste several types of premium saké, it may not be clear just what you should be looking for, especially if most of what you have been exposed to up until now was the piping hot, tasteless saké served at many Asian restaurants.

Saké has been described as having up to four hundred flavor components. Naturally, the words that we use to describe and quantify what our senses perceive are a factor of our native language. Although most often a direct correlation can be drawn, the words used in one language will convey different nuances than those used in another, so that the way saké is appraised in Japanese will definitely differ from the way it is done in English. However, the feelings and flavors behind the words are pretty much the same.

There are also different levels of appreciation. One is simply an attempt to describe what a saké tastes like in a very general sense. Another might be the effort to discern the finest and most hidden subtleties that make a particular saké unique. The range of terms and their descriptiveness will vary accordingly.

Saké taste profiles have changed quite a bit over the last thirty years, as have the preferences of consumers. Also, the overall quality level of saké has improved considerably. Before the 1960s, premium saké in the form of *ginjō-shu* was not really available on the market, although it did exist for competition purposes. Back then, saké was much less complex, so it was much simpler to assess. Saké was generally categorized as either sweet (*amakuchi*) or dry (*karakuchi*), and this classification alone served the needs of consumers. The concept of sweet versus dry is still alive today, although it alone is too general to accurately describe the complexities of today's saké.

As quality improved, more expressive terms became necessary. Enter the descriptive system of the *go-mi,* or five flavors. This historical and culturally rooted approach offers more descriptive latitude than the *amakuchi-karakuchi* distinction alone. The five flavors of the *go-mi* are *karami* (dryness), *amami* (sweetness), *nigami* (bitterness), *sanmi* (acidity), and *shibumi* (somewhere between astringency and tartness). Naturally, there are limitations to this system as well. For example, *karami* and *amami* are mutually exclusive in the minds of most, and the vague term *shibumi* is more of a perception based on other factors than a flavor itself. However, there are many other nuances and countless other flavor elements that need to be described in today's saké.

Beyond flavor, the fragrance of today's saké can be complex and varied. Here again, the vocabulary of the past simply would not be enough to do justice to the craft.

One flavor concept that has received recent attention in the wine world, but that has long been a part of saké assessment, is that of *umami*. The literal translation of the word *umami* is "deliciousness." *Umami* is the element in food or drink that evokes a response such as, "Mmmm, this is good. I think I'll have a bit more." It is more often found in full-bodied saké than in lighter, drier varieties. *Umami* is partially related to the amino acid content, which is sometimes listed on the label of premium saké.

What to Look For

When tasting saké, it is important to assess it in relation to other saké. To taste a saké while mentally comparing it to, for example, white wine, would not only disappoint, it would be unfair. It is also important to have a standard of comparison, which calls for tasting many different types of saké over time. This allows one to develop a sense of what is good in saké, and what is less so.

Qualities prized in saké in Japan may not be prized elsewhere. In particular, consumers in the United States tend to prefer bigger, bolder, livelier flavor and fragrance profiles. This is evident in the adaptation of European wine and beer styles for the United States market. Craft beer and wine made in the United States are often more assertive, ostentatious, and vivacious than their overseas counterparts.

Japanese preferences in saké are toward subtle, balanced, intuitively tasty saké. This preference for gentle flavors is consistent with Japanese cuisine in general, and in preferences for tea and other culturally steeped delicacies. Naturally, there is plenty of flamboyant saké brewed in Japan as well, but for the most part, saké that is loud or bold is not exceedingly popular. Only time will tell how things will unfold in the United States and elsewhere.

Many saké labels list important numbers which help to give an indication of what the flavor profile might be like. One is the *nihonshu-do,* known unofficially in English as the Saké Meter Value, and commonly abbreviated as SMV. Basically, the SMV is the specific gravity of the saké, or the density of the saké in comparison to pure water. What it indicates, in a very vague way, is sweetness or dryness. A typical *nihonshu-do* value is usually between −3 and +10, although numbers outside of this range are possible.

Although many factors affect the sensation of sweet and dry in saké, a simple rule of thumb is that higher SMV numbers indicate drier saké, and lower SMV numbers indicate sweeter saké. A saké with an SMV of +8 usually would be quite dry, whereas a saké with a value of −1 would likely be fairly sweet. An SMV of +2 or so might be considered somewhat neutral on the sweet/dry scale.

One factor among many that affects the sensation of sweet or dry above and beyond the SMV is the saké's general acid content. Its numbers are generally in a very small range, perhaps 0.6 to 1.6, and do not have a direct correlation to anything immediately recognizable. The method of measuring is complex and fairly technical. It is enough to keep in mind that when two sakés have the same SMV, the one with the higher acidity will tend to seem a bit drier. Higher acidity also allows flavor to spread quickly across the palate.

Another number seen, but less commonly, is the amino acid content. This too hovers in a narrow range of about 0.8 to 1.3. It can suggest a bit about the flavor: if too low, the saké will taste thin; too high, and the saké will have too many off-flavors. Note that these parameters are only guidelines, and in the end will tell you far less than your own palate will. Tasting for yourself is the only truly valid way to assess a saké.

COMING TO YOUR SENSES

Ultimately, nothing can replace your own palate, preferences, and experience in determining if a particular saké suits you. Naturally, several senses are used to assess the attributes of a saké.

Eyes

Saké ranges from transparent to amber in color. Modern day filtering allows this to be controlled to a precise degree, and often is an expression of the preferences of the brewer. Regardless of whether a saké is completely clear or a lovely straw yellow, it should have a decent luster to the appearance. Dull looking saké is not likely to have been well cared for, or well brewed in the first place. Aged saké represents a slight deviation from this rule, as it can often be dark yellow-brown in appearance. Still, it should not be cloudy or laced with sediment.

Nigori-zake, however, is an exception to all of this. It is deliberately left cloudy, which is precisely its appeal. Note that the cloudiness of a nigori-zake should not be confused with the cloudiness that results from nama-zake (unpasteurized saké) that has not been properly stored. If not kept refrigerated, nama-zake can essentially spoil, and it develops a cloudiness that is more suspended than grainy in nature, moving within the bottle similarly to the way the red liquid moves inside a lava lamp.

Nose

Some saké is fragrant, whereas other saké is not, and fragrance is not directly related to quality or grade. In many regions of Japan, an overly fragrant saké is considered too dainty and wine-like, and therefore a diversion from what true saké should be. At the same time, over the last few years countless yeast strains have been isolated and cultivated precisely for the purpose of creating more fragrant saké.

Some saké aromas are light and barely perceptible, some seductive, others downright loud. Some rise in wisps and are gone, and others have staying power to last the whole glass. Flowers, nuts, fresh fruit, ripe fruit, rice, yeast, and even grassy and herbal smells are all fair game for a saké fragrance. It is important to consider, too, how the fragrance fits in with the flavor. Is it too strong, too weak, disjointed? Or does it seem connected and blend naturally?

Palate

The way that a saké strikes your palate is called the *kuchi-atari*. What is the first impression it leaves? Is most of the flavor up front, or does the saké make more of a quiet entrance? Is it bold, crisp, and assertive, or soft and demure? Is the acidity so high it awakens you upon entry, or is it hardly perceptible?

Mouth feel is another important attribute. Some saké is grainy and textural as it moves across the tongue. Others are light, and seem to glide about. Saké can run from viscous and chewy to billowy and effervescent. All are fine, provided they are in line with personal preferences.

Next, consider the overall hardness or softness. Saké is mostly water, and the water from which it was brewed carries its distinctions through to the final product. Is it crisp and clean, or does it absorb deeply into the palate and tongue?

Simple impressions of flavor, while thoroughly subjective, are more directly perceived. Premium *ginjō-shu* can be fruity, for example, and that fruitiness can be reminiscent of melons, strawberries, peaches, persimmons, prunes, apples, and citrus, just for starters. Some saké is more rice-like, occasionally with subtle undertones of richness, almost like chocolate or licorice. Very often saké can taste faintly reminiscent of nuts, grass, and flowers.

Finish

How does the saké work its way across your palate? Does it beat a fat, wide path, or a narrow lane? Does it spread into each and every crevice of your mouth, or does it gently meander without disturbing the surroundings any more than necessary? Is it full of interesting flavors and sensations, or stripped down to the bare essentials of flavor? Some saké approaches quietly, then explodes into flavor. Some disappears from the mouth and throat almost instantaneously, others linger in both flavor and fragrance. Often, it's the acidity, rather than the flavor, that tingles long after the saké is gone.

SERVING SAKÉ

Saké should be approached the way any fine sipping beverage is approached. One would no sooner make a cocktail with a fine saké than one would mix a fine wine with juice or soda. Mixing or flavoring will only mask or obscure the original flavor profile of the saké. Certainly, people should drink what they like, and if flavored saké and saké cocktails are appealing then by all means they should be enjoyed. If such variations help facilitate a fondness for proper saké tasting, all the better. However, saké cocktails and the like will not be addressed here.

Temperature

The pervading image of saké is that of a beverage to be consumed hot. Historically, this is accurate, for until about fifty years ago, most saké on the market was not as delicate in flavor, and warming tended to mask the rough spots. Over the last several decades, thanks to technology and experience, saké has changed dramatically. To warm most saké now would be to eliminate the fruitiness and subtle, layered flavors—precisely the qualities it was brewed to exude.

Most good saké should be consumed slightly chilled, although there are, of course, exceptions. As with any fine beverage, even a small change in temperature will bring out certain characteristics, and it can be extremely interesting to notice the changes in flavor as a chilled saké slowly warms up a bit.

Admittedly, warm saké has a unique sensory appeal, and less-than-sterling saké can be warmed without harm. There is also an increasing number of premium saké created specifically to taste better warmed—but not too hot. None of these premium saké should be heated higher than one hundred to one hundred five degrees Fahrenheit (forty degrees Celcius), as the flavor would be smothered. But in the end, if you truly prefer sake warm, don't let anyone talk you out of it.

Vessels

Traditionally, saké is drunk from small cups called *o-chokko,* or slightly larger, more artistic versions called *guinomi.* It is poured from earthen or ceramic flasks called *tokkuri.* The shape of the *tokkuri,* with its tapered neck, helps keep saké warm.

Most *o-chokko* and *guinomi* are relatively simple, with wide mouths, but there is little consistency in shape. Some are straight-sided, some flare out gently, and a few taper in. What matters is the style and quality of the pottery, and the cup's weight and texture. Japan has a distinguished history of fine ceramics. Some pieces are fairly refined, but others are simpler and rougher, indicative of the earth from which they were created, and may be glazed or unglazed. Everything from the surface roughness to the thickness of the rim will affect the experience. *O-chokko, guinomi,* and *tokkuri* are some of the most artistic and interesting pottery forms made in Japan. The saké experience is a sensory one, and should indeed go beyond taste and smell to equally involve sight and feel. Proper *o-chokko, guinomi,* and *tokkuri* are instrumental in helping achieve this.

There is a cultural explanation for the small size of *o-chokko.* Saké, and alcohol in general, has for centuries served as a social lubricant in Japan. One well-known custom is that of refilling the cups of your drinking companions. Smaller cups lead to the need for more frequent refilling. This deeply entrenched custom is one reason that wine glasses or similar stemware have never been used to any great degree with saké.

What should you use to drink saké at home, should you not have proper *tokkuri* and *o-chokko*? A simple tumbler works very well, and a martini glass, though somewhat extravagant, can also be nice. Wine glasses, while focusing the fragrance, often have the effect of disassociating that fragrance from the flavor profile, putting too much space between them.

The tax department in Japan maintains a nationwide team of professional tasters, who assess saké in government-sponsored competitions. The tax department sponsors such competitions to encourage brewers to constantly improve their product, which leads to more tax revenue. These highly trained tasters use either a 180-milliliter amber tumbler or a white porcelain glass with several blue concentric circles in a bullseye pattern on the bottom to help discern clarity. Smaller versions of this tumbler are popular in saké pubs.

Another traditional vessel is a small wooden box, or *masu*. Originally, the *masu* was a measure of rice, basically one meal's worth. It holds about 180 milliliters, which is considered one standard drink. Until a few decades ago, *masu* were commonly used for drinking saké, especially among men at local saké pubs. Often a pinch of salt was placed on one corner as a palate clearer. Even today, the *masu* and salt serve as a symbol for saké drinking. However, the cedar from which the *masu* is made imparts a scent and flavor of its own, which can change the perception of a fine saké. Thirty or forty years ago, saké was sweeter, rougher, and vastly different than saké today. It could easily stand up to a *masu,* as well as the pinch of salt. Except for special events like festivals and weddings, saké is no longer drunk from a *masu,* at least not directly. Many saké pubs will place a glass in a *masu* in an attempt to protect the inherent flavor of the saké, while maintaining a bit of tradition as well.

Part II

Directory of Japanese and American Saké

Any saké enthusiast worth his rice will want to know about the 137 saké reviewed here. Most are available in the United States, and those that are not currently available show great promise for becoming so in the near future. Efforts have been made to present an objective, fair, across-the-board list of saké suitable for sampling, representative of all styles, all regions of Japan, as well as the six saké brewed in the United States, and all price ranges. These include commercially well-known brands as well as some excellent brands known only to connoisseurs.

I have attempted to introduce saké about which it would behoove any saké enthusiast to know. These may be from large, well-known brewers of consistent quality, or from tiny breweries of outstanding quality that one can only get in Japan, or even perhaps only in the region where they are brewed. Should you find your way to Japan for any reason or any length of time, these are brands you will want to know about.

This list is not by any stretch of the imagination comprehensive, or even remotely representative of all that is available. In fact, the list has been slightly biased toward saké already for sale in the United States. There are countless wonderful saké. If you come across one that is not listed here, please do not assume it is not noteworthy, tasty, or well-known. It is simply a matter of having to draw the line somewhere, and creating a cross-section of the saké world.

Still, the saké reviewed herein is all better than average saké. In light of establishing saké as a premium beverage in an already-crowded premium beverage market, it does not make sense to present boring or less-than-impressive saké. This is not to say that gentler, less-impacting saké is not worth drinking, but the ability to impress takes priority in this list.

NOTES ON THE RATINGS

Each saké listed here is followed by a numerical ranking. Such ratings are a double-edged sword, and I have applied them grudgingly. It would be truly unfortunate if a reader were to avoid a saké based on a numerical rating here, for these numbers are little more than an expression of how one feels about a particular saké at a particular time. Too much subjectivity is involved in making such an assessment. What are your personal likes? Are you tasting only one saké or several? If several, in what order? What food, if any, are you having? What is the atmosphere? Will you have one glass or several? What physical and emotional state are you in? There are just too many factors to make numerical scores absolute. It is really up to each individual to determine for himself or herself how "good" or "not good" a saké is.

However, these numbers can be useful in that they provide a place to start. Although nothing can replace your own personal experience and your palate when it comes to assessing the merits of a saké, an arrow at the crossroads sure comes in handy.

Each rating number is based on a very simple assessment of several facets of the overall profile, including flavor, fragrance, lack of off-flavors, character, overall pleasingness, and—most importantly—balance.

Here's how the numbers work:

93+.................Excellent
90-93...............Highly recommended
86-90...............Recommended
81-85...............Good
75-80...............Fair
Below 75............Poor

READING SAKÉ LABELS

In saké made by the six breweries in the United States, the type and grade are clearly marked on the label. Although the special terminology may not be defined, at least the wording is in English.

Japanese saké labels, on the other hand, can be problematic if you cannot read the characters describing the various types or the *meigara* (brand name). Although there are regulations as to what information needs to be on the label, there are none about where on the label such information should be placed, nor about legibility. By law, the back label of saké imported from Japan into the United States must be in English, with the name of the saké and the grade printed legibly.

The two main pieces of information on a label are the *meigara* and the grade, such as *junmai-shu* or *ginjō-shu*. Unfortunately, these are not located in the same place on all bottles, nor are they uniformly sized. Thus, knowing where to look—as well as what to look for—can be problematic.

The best advice is to try to remember the characters for premium saké and to look for those characters somewhere on the label. Often, this information is provided on restaurant menus and retail shop shelves. As the United States opens up to the imported Japanese saké market, and as U.S. saké brewers provide information, consumer understanding will improve along with brand recognition and experience.

HOW TO USE THIS DIRECTORY

In the list that follows, large producers are mixed in with the small ones, as well as the six brewers based in the United States. All are represented with no bias, in strict alphabetical order.

Each listing adheres to the following basic format. The main *meigara,* or brand name, is first, often followed by a sub-brand name. This is followed by the type classification. Finally, the prefecture (and its location as indicated on the small map at the bottom of each page) where the saké was brewed is listed. For saké brewed in the United States, the city and state of the brewery are given.

AMA NO TO

"UMASHINE"

Junmai ginjō-shu

Ama no To means "Heaven's Door;" it has a young feel, which begins with mild green apples in the nose, and continues into the refreshing but settled flavor which comes knock, knock, knocking on your palate.

Overall: This is a very well constructed saké, delicately put together, with incredible balance among the flavors.

Rating: 90

Akita, Japan

AMANOZAKE

"KĪSSHŌ"

Ginjō-shu

A lively but mature nose, with lots of esters manifesting themselves in strawberries and bananas; an even more settled and mature flavor; very quickly disappearing tail, interesting for such a rich saké.

Overall: A bit reminiscent of aged saké in its earthy edges, with a subtle richness—*umami*—that makes you come back for more.

Rating: 89

Osaka, Japan

AMERICAN PACIFIC RIM KI-IPPON
Tokubetsu junmai-shu

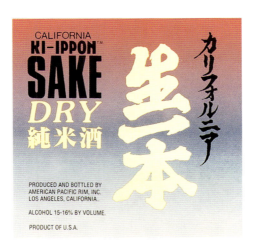

Mossy and vegetation-like facets across the flavor; long tail.

Overall: Brewed in the United States, this saké has a somewhat heavy *junmai* flavor without the *junmai* acidity.

Rating: 75

Vernon, California

ASABIRAKI
Junmai-shu

A bit drier and more slender than most saké from the Iwate region, which tend to be medium-bodied and neutral or gently sweet, with nice texture. Decent fragrance of apples and flowers, faint but good for a *junmai-shu*.

Overall: This *junmai-shu* is crisp, clean, and refined, with a fairly low acid presence.

Rating: 82

Iwate, Japan

ASAHI TENYU

Junmai ginjō-shu

This saké has a wonderful nose, almost berry-like, with a bit of butter, persimmons, and figs. This motley assortment of fragrances is also very apparent in the flavor, on a somewhat dry foundation. A nice tartness in the tail.

Overall: One of the best reasons for recommending this saké is that it is wonderful served warm. Not too hot, just a gentle warming, and all kinds of charms become more apparent.

Rating: 88

Shimane, Japan

AYAKIKU

Junmai ginjō-shu

All Ayakiku saké shares a very strong thread of distinction, likely from the fact that it is made with the same rice, Oseto, which is not all that common; flowery and citrus-laced nose.

Overall: Solid flavor with comparatively strong bitter and tart elements, and definite earthy undertones.

Rating: 84

Kagawa, Japan

Azuma Ichi

Junmai-shu

A hint of walnuts and chestnuts lurking in the background, with a slight cherry essence. Decent viscosity and pleasing mouth feel. Some of the higher grades of saké made by this *kura* are truly outstanding. All maintain a wonderful purity of flavor, with a marked absence of off-flavors.

Overall: Slightly dry, with a nice, full acidity bolstering the flavor.

Rating: 91

Saga, Japan

AZUMA RIKISHI

Junmai ginjō-shu

A tanginess in the back of the palate creeps slowly forward as you sip. Very faint floral and rice-like fragrance draws you into the settled flavor; acidity, not all that apparent, seems to do its flavor-spreading work in the background.

Overall: A fairly mellow saké leaning ever so slightly toward the sweet side of things.

Rating: 87

Tochigi, Japan

Biwa no Chōjū

Junmai ginjō-shu

Mild tangerines and strawberries in the nose lead into a fairly tight flavor profile; extremely layered and complex, with a full, rich flavor that is diced up nicely by a pervasive acidity.

Overall: Interesting enough to drink on its own, without food. Biwa no Chōjū comes into its own when cool or chilled.

Rating: 93

Shiga, Japan

BIZEN SAKÉ NO HITOSUJI
Junmai ginjō-shu

Bizen Saké no Hitosuji is made from Ōmachi, an old saké rice that grows best in Okayama. Solid and well constructed fragrance, spicy and green; fairly dry flavor with lots of richness and earthiness, but few off-flavors.

Overall: This saké (and nearly every saké brewed in Okayama) almost always tastes good warm.

Rating: 92

Okayama, Japan

Chiyo no Kame
"Ginga Tetsudo"
Junmai daiginjō-shu

Aged a full ten years at temperatures close to zero, this is a saké with well-rounded edges and flavors that blend into each other, with just a touch of the musty, tangy elements that are common in saké aged at higher temperatures.

Overall: Although wonderful chilled, it will stand up to some mild warming as well. Understandably a bit expensive and hard to get, but you only live once.

Rating: 89

Ehime, Japan

CHIYO NO SONO

"YAMAGA"

Junmui-shu

This saké boasts a fascinating flavor profile; the nose is somewhat peppery but laced with faint melon fruits. The acid-spawned tartness lingers in the tail, holding a bitter note ever so lightly and pleasantly to finish.

Overall: Sweet and slightly bitter elements duke it out across your tongue in a flavor profile that was obviously very deliberately and artistically crafted.

Rating: 90

Kumamoto, Japan

DAISHICHI
"KIMOTO"
Junmai-shu·

Lovely nose laced with definite nutty facets, suffused with a gentle sweetness. The flavor, too, has a heavy-sweet platform on top of which a lighter, melting rice richness rests.

Overall: The flow of the flavors along the tongue makes this memorable and unique, very characteristic of Fukushima saké.

Rating: 88

Fukushima, Japan

DENSHU

Junmai-shu

An amazing rice flavor, solid and tightly put together, with a distinctive richness far from cloying; elegantly constructed with a delicate tone; nose is of flowers and distant chestnuts. There are *ginjō-shu* and *daiginjō-shu* versions that are lighter and more fragrant, but still toe the rice-laden line.

Overall: This is a saké-drinker's saké. It perennially tops lists of favorites, and is great when served slightly warmed.

Rating: 93

Aomori, Japan

DEWAZAKURA

"IKKOU"

Junmai-shu

Dry and settled, with some nuts and grass in the background, but with a slightly sweet note riding on top; good acidity disseminates the tail nicely. The fragrance is "now you smell it, now you don't," laced with a bit of banana and chestnut.

Overall: With a lively and clear tone to the flavor, this saké works well decently chilled, but should lend itself to experimental warming as well.

Rating: 88

Yamagata, Japan

DEWAZURU

"GIN IPPON"

Junmai ginjō-shu

Nice, hard water helps this brewery create some sterling saké that stand out from others in the Akita region. A refined, sharp package of flavors and sensations is coaxed along by very slight fruit fragrances like cantaloupe and peach. Dewazuru also makes a fine *daiginjō-shu* called Hishō no Mai, which is lighter and a bit fruitier than this *ginjō-shu*.

Overall: Gin Ippon is solidly constructed, with very clear lines of delineation among the flavors.

Rating: 88

Akita, Japan

ECHIGO TSURUKAME

Tokubetsu junmai-shu

Light and crisp, with a fairly sharp, clean edge to the flavor; more of a rice nose than a fruit essence; slightly fuller body than most Niigata saké, which are usually more slender and dry.

Overall: Very solidly constructed and well brewed, this saké will stand up to most lighter fare and maintain its presence.

Rating: 83

Niigata, Japan

EIKO FUJI

Junmai-shu

A slight sweetness buoyed by faint banana and berry fruit essences in the nose are most apparent at or just below room temperature. Eiko Fuji makes a wide range of wonderful saké, including a great *nama-zake* and a different *daiginjō-shu* called "Hitori Yogari."

Overall: Light for a *junmai-shu*. Although the acidity is average for this type of saké, it is not all that apparent in the flavor, allowing instead a more mellowed softness to exude.

Rating: 86

Yamagata, Japan

EISEN

Junmai-shu

Strawberries and apples mingle in the nose, which is faint but in equilibrium with the flavor. *Junmai*-like acidity helps spread the flavor well. Higher grades of Eisen saké become somewhat lighter and fruitier, but maintain the same basic essence and almost non-distinctive mellowness.

Overall: Compared to other saké in this region, Eisen is a bit dry. It has a settled, balanced aspect to its overall mellowness that is relaxing. It strikes the palate softly and smoothly. Works well with mildly flavored food.

Rating: 85

Fukushima, Japan

FUCHU HOMARE

"WATARIBUNE"

Junmai daiginjō-shu

Made from a saké rice that had all but disappeared, but was revived by this *kura* and the rice farmers of the area; rich and full, with green apples and tangerines in the nose. The flavor unfolds wonderfully with a bit of decanting to reveal an actively dancing array of fruit and rice elements.

Overall: A truly outstanding *daiginjō-shu,* well worth the price. Not much is brewed, so it may be hard to get outside of the Kanto area (near Tokyo).

Rating: 93

Ibaraki, Japan

FUKUCHO

"BIHO"

Junmai ginjō-shu

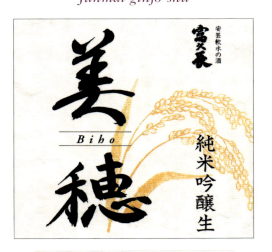

Wonderful fragrance, fruity and rich, with depth and character; the flavor itself is fairly light and quite absorbing as it trickles by the tongue. Although not a session saké, one glass will indeed impress all comers.

Overall: Fukucho takes a fairly soft approach to the palate, as is typical of Hiroshima saké and its soft water. Room temperature or just below is best here.

Rating: 90

Hiroshima, Japan

FUKUMASAMUNE

"MIZUHO"

Junmai ginjō-shu

Faint rice and nuts with low acidity form the main pillar of flavor, with a slight sweetness rising around that. The tail retreats slowly, leaving a very pleasant wake. Fukumasamune has a wide range of products, including Kyōka, which has a fuller, more grounded flavor and slightly nuttier facets to it.

Overall: Gentle and mild, with an unassuming flavor and light melons dancing in the nose.

Rating: 85

Ishikawa, Japan

FUKUNISHIKI

Junmai-shu

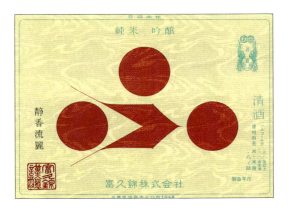

Nose is just a tad astringent with evident acidity, not much flower or fruit—somewhat typical of Hyogo saké. Good impact on the palate, with a full richness that goes diving into nooks and crannies. Acidity comes roaring back pleasantly to get you near the end.

Overall: Mellow, rice-like flavor.

Rating: 85

Hyogo, Japan

FUMOTOI
"HONKARA MADOKA"
Junmai-shu

This saké is made using the *kimoto* method, in which more wild bacteria than usual are allowed to enter the yeast starter. This creates a stronger flavor, with sweet, bitter, and tart elements much more prevalent.

Overall: Sharp, crisp approach to the palate, with an immediate bitter tone rising. This soon fades, allowing some astringency to appear, but it all smoothes out to nothingness in a fun finish.

Rating: 86

Yamagata, Japan

GASSAN

Junmai ginjō-shu

A lightly fruity and lightly sweet persona underlined by a good acidity. Strikes the palate in a lively, zesty way, with a nutty, full flavor in the center. Persimmon and peach pervade. A nice, long, but balanced, tail keeps pulling you along.

Overall: The slightly heavy richness is typical of saké from the Shimane area. This is nice ever so slightly chilled.

Rating: 89

Shimane, Japan

GEKKEIKAN

Ginjō-shu

Soft and balanced, with a melting quality that defines Kyoto saké; plums and just a bit of paper in the nose. A full, grainy richness is evident through the finish.

Overall: Although Gekkeikan is the largest brewer in Japan, they still pay attention to the small stuff.

Rating: 78

Kyoto, Japan

GEKKEIKAN

Junmai ginjō-shu

Not as soft as their Japan-brewed saké, but then again, they do not have the Kyoto water. Clean and dry overall, with a full presence and a grainy mouth feel.

Overall: Solid and clean, mildly fragrant.

Rating: 76

Folsom, California

GINBAN

"BANSHU GINBAN 50"

Junmai ginjō-shu

Ginban is in the top forty brewers as measured by output. Although this saké is "mass produced" by most standards, its quality is very high. The "50" in the name refers to the rice-milling rate, or *seimai-buai.* A peppery and rice-like nose leads to a grainy flavor that expands to fill the whole mouth.

Overall: This is one of those rare saké that is very good cold, at room temperature, and warmed—albeit significantly different at each temperature. A low acidity makes it very versatile.

Rating: 85

Toyama, Japan

GOKYO

Junmai-shu

Gokyo exhibits the wonderful quality of having an *oku-bukai* flavor (meaning deep and layered) that always seems to present another aspect from the background. The tail leaves slightly bitter and acidic notes as it slowly fades.

Overall: A mellow, nutty nose that fades a bit too quickly for some, and a full, very balanced flavor.

Rating: 90

Yamaguchi, Japan

GOSHUN

"IKEDA-SAKÉ"

This very no-nonsense *kura* does not state the class of its saké, preferring to use the old names that were active before the "Special Class, First Class, Second Class" system ended in 1989. Although this saké is likely of *honjōzō-shu* class, it is not on the label; faint fragrance, imperceptible to many; more sweet than dry compared to most saké today, but balanced and just right.

Overall: Not overpowering in any particular way, but with an almost cerebrally satisfying flavor. Hard to find outside Osaka, but well worth knowing about.

Rating: 89

Osaka, Japan

GOZENSHU

"MIMISAKU"

Junmai-shu

Brewed in the prefecture where wonderful Ōmachi saké rice grows best, by one of the few remaining *tōji* of the Bichu school. A nice flower and nectar nose, and a wide but elegant flavor, with some vegetation and smoke. Flavor fades slowly in the tail.

Overall: Great richness, diffused by the pervading acidity.

Rating: 87

Okayama, Japan

HAKKAISAN
Junmai ginjō-shu

Fairly crisp overall and quite dry; very clean, too; faintly sweet. Hakkaisan makes some higher grade *ginjō-shu* that, while expensive, are outstanding if you are fond of that dry, ultra-light style.

Overall: A well-known brand of classic Niigata style, dry and light; richer than most saké from this area, and indeed most saké from this *kura*.

Rating: 88

Niigata, Japan

HAKUSAN

Junmai ginjō-shu

Very soft and mild *ginjō-shu*; nice rice-like tones to the background, with rougher, earthy tones up front; mild, grassy fragrance.

Overall: Gentle, straightforward, and earthy.

Rating: 76

Napa, California

HAKUSHIKA

Junmai-shu

Mild flavor, with an earthy presence in the background that gives it a settled structure. A crisp, dry entry opens up gently, revealing a faint vanilla-like tone in the recesses. Very quiet nose, as is typical for saké from this region, and an overall masculine dryness that relaxes and invites.

Overall: Simple and straightforward, but not overly so.

Rating: 84

Hyogo, Japan

Harushika

"Cho-karakuchi"

Junmai-shu

The name "Cho-karakuchi" means "super dry," and dry it is, but not so much that it is out of balance; moderate fragrance of nuts and rice; very little fruit.

Overall: Very clean and smooth on the tongue; goes down very easily and cleanly with no trace of off-flavors in the palate or finish.

Rating: 83

Nara, Japan

HATSUKAME

Junmai ginjō-shu

Nice fruity nose, melons and citrus, with a chestnut fragrance (compliments of the *kōji*) dancing in the background; lively especially in the center and end of the palate; clean tail.

Overall: A light saké with low acidity that comes off as sweet at first, but later dries out as the flavor spreads around.

Rating: 89

Shizuoka, Japan

HITAKAMI

Junmai ginjō-shu

Light and faint fruitiness to the nose, mostly comprised of strawberries and bananas; mouth feel is soft, with no one flavor overpowering. Gentle flavors and fragrances continue to jump out as the saké makes its way around your mouth.

Overall: As nothing about this saké is overly assertive, it works well with a wide range of food, and is best served slightly chilled.

Rating: 90

Miyagi, Japan

HITORI MUSUME

"SAYAKA"

Ginjō-shu

A saké for fans of dry saké, clean and crisp from beginning to end, with good acidity. The nose is understandably faint, as too much would not jibe with the bone-dry flavor.

Overall: Nice saké to match with food of a slightly stronger character. Better served cool than warmed.

Rating: 83

Ibaraki, Japan

ICHINOKURA

"MUKANSA"

Junmai-shu

Nice citrus and cantaloupe nose, short-lived though it might be; flavor is not overflowing with distinction but is nonetheless pleasing, and Ichinokura is easy to drink; nice, expanding mouth feel with a moderate acidity.

Overall: A good choice for warming as it retains its smoothness at higher temperatures.

Rating: 82

Miyagi, Japan

ISOJIMAN
Tokubetsu honjōzō-shu

A fascinating nose of a whole array of fruit and nuts blended seamlessly to create one gently wafting fragrance; crystal-clear but lively flavor profile, layered and active. Isojiman makes *ginjō-shu* and *daiginjō-shu* saké (they make nothing lower than *honjōzō-shu* grade), but it is not necessary to go that far.

Overall: Excellent—not to be missed. Wonderful enough to satisfy endlessly.

Rating: 95

Shizuoka, Japan

JŪYONDAI

Junmai ginjō-shu

Fine, very balanced fragrance; mostly lighter fruit like strawberries and apples, but grounded in a flowery and grassy anchor; light, vibrant, and complex flavor profile opens and spreads expansively. Layer upon layer of new tones and facets unfold with each passing moment.

Overall: Fully absorbing—easily the most popular saké among young saké drinkers today in Japan.

Rating: 94

Yamagata, Japan

KAIUN

Junmai ginjō-shu

The fragrance is billowing and vivacious, but not at all overpowering. The flavor is light but active, layered with a touch of peppery goodness. Light oranges and strawberries seem most prominent, but a background of nuts and slightly bitter elements helps keep it grounded.

Overall: Tightly constructed flavor profile with a very layered and complex unfolding.

Rating: 94

Shizuoka, Japan

KAMOIZUMI

Junmai ginjō-shu

Fascinating and unique, with a much earthier, woodier flavor than most; bitter and acidic notes stabilize the slightly dry but heavy flavor. A gorgeous golden color suffuses this saké, enhancing the sipping experience greatly. The woody and tart nose is similar to the flavor.

Overall: Balanced and appetizing, this is a great saké to serve warm.

Rating: 93

Hiroshima, Japan

KARIHO
"ROKUSHŪ"
Ginjō-shu

Rokushū has a somewhat full body, but with the rougher edges polished away, leaving a light saké with a good amount of content. Leaning to the dry side, the flavor is laced with various elements of nuts, rice, and even a trace of richer fruit.

Overall: A versatile saké indeed, with a charming liveliness that comes out at room temperature, and a calming crispness most apparent when cool or chilled.

Rating: 88

Akita, Japan

Kenbishi

"Tokusen"

One of the most famous saké in Japan, with a slightly tart nose, and good acidity to liven things up. Its symbol, two black diamond-like shapes, is equally famous. The *kura* and its brewing are very traditional and secretive—no classification is designated for this saké.

Overall: Mellow and confident; rather sweet for saké from the Nada region, although relatively dry.

Rating: 82

Hyogo, Japan

KIKUHIME

Junmai ginjō-shu

This *ginjō-shu* has a nose full of plums and prunes, well aerated, with a flowery, almost grass-like touch. The palate is at first just slightly dry and crisp, but the subtle dance of fruit flavors and sharp tones later is wonderful.

Overall: This is a highly sought-after saké, from a very enthusiastic *kura* that uses one hundred percent saké rice in all of its saké; a true rarity.

Rating: 88

Ishikawa, Japan

KIKUMASAMUNE

Honjōzō-shu

Nice dry flavor with a touch of wild acidity and bitter background; nice fruity, acid-based flavor dances on an earthy, coffee bean-laced backdrop; sour mash in nose, due likely to proprietary yeast.

Overall: Kikumasamune is the sixth largest brewer in Japan, but perhaps the one large brewer with the most distinction. This is a great example of good saké from a mass producer.

Rating: 85

Hyogo, Japan

KIKUSUI

Junmai ginjō-shu

Dry, but not as much as most Niigata saké, and not as light; a bit more flavor, with a lemony background and a nice acidity opening the palate up front; a slightly lingering finish has more fruit in it than at the beginning of the palate.

Overall: A very popular Niigata brand, very easy to drink, and best served a few degrees below room temperature.

Rating: 82

Niigata, Japan

Kikuyoi

Tokubetsu honjōzō-shu

Balanced, with an underlying richness; the faint fruit essences like strawberries and bananas in the nose pull you into a gentle and mature after-flavor. Very reasonably priced for all this flavor, too.

Overall: Young and slightly brash. A lively, light, easy-to-drink session saké from a small, enthusiastic, committed *kura*.

Rating: 91

Shizuoka, Japan

KINPAI YORO

Junmai daiginjō-shu

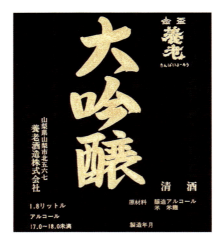

A very tiny *kura* brews this saké in unreasonably small batches, with remarkable consistency and tasty results. Good acidity and wonderful mouth feel create a richness in both fragrance and flavor that may be overpowering to light saké fans, but just perfect to others.

Overall: A very full-bodied saké, bursting with ripe fruit and other lively flavors. You'll be lucky to find it, though.

Rating: 87

Yamanashi, Japan

KIRIN

Junmai daiginjō-shu

A soft, inviting saké with a classy harmony of flavors that unfolds across your palate, delivering a refined manifestation of fine Niigata "Koshi Hikari" rice; not an overly loud saké, fairly demure in its presentation, with a quiet fragrance of rice and gentle flowers; a very clean tail that fades in the blink of an eye.

Overall: Best served fairly cool to enjoy the clean, subtle flavors.

Rating: 88

Niigata, Japan

KIRINZAN

Junmai-shu

A well-known saké that typifies the *tanrei-karakuchi* (light and dry) Niigata style quite well, but still goes a step or two in the direction of individuality; within the dryness, a faintly soft and sweet element spreads quietly like an undercurrent.

Overall: Overchilling this saké can destroy it, as can warming. Room temperature may be best.

Rating: 83

Niigata, Japan

KIYOIZUMI

Tokubetsu junmai-shu

A rich but subtle flavor of rice and fermenting fruit, with a touch of hazelnut; a well-balanced softness keeps all this under wraps at first, but it unfolds nicely with a bit of time. This *kura* led the way in reviving the rice called Kame no Ō, and created a *daiginjō-shu* from it which has the same name.

Overall: Not as dry as most saké from the Niigata region, and certainly more impacting and flavorful.

Rating: 89

Niigata, Japan

KOKURYŪ

Junmai ginjō-shu

The varied and unique fragrance, characterized by gently dueling fruit essences against a nutty and cinnamon-toned backdrop, indicates a lot about this wonderful saké. The flavor is subtly layered with deep recesses of richer flavors, a combination of autumn fruit and bitter elements, like tree bark and herbs.

Overall: A wonderful blend of flavors with lovely balance. Kokuryū is one of the great cost performers of the saké world.

Rating: 94

Fukui, Japan

Kokushi Muso
Tokubetsu junmai-shu

Generally neutral, neither too sweet nor too dry, but with pleasing acidity that makes its presence felt in the middle of the action. The tail is quick to vanish, clean and tidy, but quiet in its exit.

Overall: A calm, clean, and comparatively mellow saké, just right for a *junmai-shu,* with a solid core of content.

Rating: 84

Hokkaido, Japan

KORO

Junmai ginjō-shu

Citrus fruit and persimmons vie in the prominent nose, and remain throughout the duration of the session. A light, fruity initial palate fades into a touch of bitterness and good astringency later, which pervade the rather thick, fat flavor.

Overall: A fun saké, very lively and fruity—memorable indeed.

Rating: 92

Kumamoto, Japan

Koshigoi

Junmai-shu

Brewed with water that comes literally gushing up from a spring across the street, the saké has a slightly nutty fragrance laced with a bit of honey. The flavor is interesting: basically full and rich, but with pockets of softness and delicate, permeating flavors.

Overall: Well-blended flavors and an effective but mild acidic touch.

Rating: 87

Chiba, Japan

KOSHI NO HAKURO

Tokubetsu junmai-shu

A nice melon-laced nose suffused by a clean acidity; the tail is fairly clean, leaving just a touch of acidity behind.

Overall: Flavor is just on the heavy and full side for Niigata saké, but may be on the light side for a *junmai-shu*. Even so, there is a decent richness (*umami*) present.

Rating: 88

Niigata, Japan

Koshi no Kanbai

Tokubetsu honjōzō-shu

When the *jizake* (micro-brewed saké from the boonies) boom hit Japan in the late 1970s, Koshi no Kanbai emerged in front, and retains that image today even though the company has expanded to become a comparatively large brewer. Very dry and clean; slight vanilla fragrance; very clean tail.

Overall: Quite likely the most famous saké in Japan. Fans of light, dry saké will love it. High grades of Koshi no Kanbai can be expensive, so be careful.

Rating: 90

Niigata, Japan

KOTSUTSUMI

Junmai-shu

Gentle nose with butter, nuts, and apples all faintly present; creamy, relaxed, and mellow flavor with banana elements fades into a quickly disappearing tail; only slightly dry, and the soft water buffers that a bit as well. This *kura* makes good use of the yeast known as Association #10, notable in the apple-toned nose.

Overall: Wonderfully quiet and intuitively appreciated saké.

Rating: 92

Hyogo, Japan

Kubota

"Senjū"

Tokubetsu honjōzō-shu

Kubota is another place that rode the *jizake* boom to stardom when it placed Niigata saké on the map in the late 1970s and early 1980s. It also brews the Asahiyama brand. This saké has not a hint of an off flavor, just a slight bitterness loitering in the undercurrent to keep the profile grounded.

Overall: Very dry and clean, as crisp and light as a saké can get.

Rating: 89

Niigata, Japan

KUMONOI

"MEIJŌ"

Junmai daiginjō-shu

A positively regal feel to the ripe apple-laced nose; delicate and layered, with the softness blending those layers together. Light fruit resides on the surface of the even flavor, with faint chestnuts and a touch of citrus in the background.

Overall: The character changes drastically as it goes from chilled to room temperature, although it shouldn't be served any warmer than that.

Rating: 88

Fukui, Japan

Kuroushi

Junmai ginjō-shu

This saké, over the past three or four years, has risen to immense popularity, basically out of nowhere. Not that it doesn't deserve it—it does. It has a light, layered, and complex flavor, blessed with very light fruit essences and a rice-flavored foundation.

Overall: Clean and complex in structure—very good indeed.

Rating: 92

Wakayama, Japan

KUSUDAMA

Junmai-shu

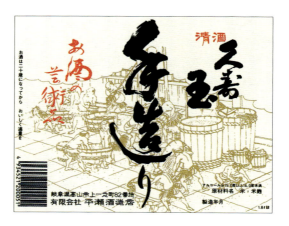

Slightly melon-laced fragrance, bootstrapped by a nice acidity; clean flavor overall, but with a nicely full profile, mildly sweet; the acidity distributes the fine mouth feel evenly and quickly.

Overall: Serving just below room temperature optimizes the flavors.

Rating: 81

Gifu, Japan

MABOROSHI
Daiginjō-shu

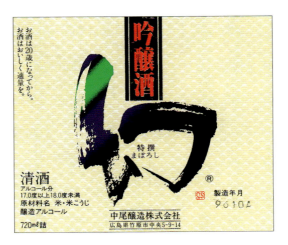

A truly excellent *daiginjō-shu,* elegant and well constructed. The maker, whose main brand is called Seikyo, uses a proprietary yeast that brings out a wonderful melon and apple nose. The flavor is not dry, rather a bit sweet and rice-like.

Overall: Sterling, clear, and well constructed. Definitely a saké to drink cool or chilled, not warmed.

Rating: 93

Hiroshima, Japan

MADONOUME

"KADEN"

Ginjō-shu

A mature-saké nose, with an almost slightly aged touch and citrus fruit notes throughout. A soft, full approach to the palate widens into a mature flavor; light in general on the palate, with a suffusing gentle acid flavor. Sweetness pervades nicely at the end.

Overall: Room temperature is a wonderful way to serve this saké.

Rating: 83

Saga, Japan

MAIHIME

"KI-IPPON"

Junmai-shu

This is a deep saké, and beneath the surface is suffusing softness and clean flavor; very faint citrus-like nose. Maihime also makes a *futsū-shu* that is calm and confident, and very easy to drink. Higher grades of saké here are soft, subdued, and gently fragrant.

Overall: Slightly on the dry side, although this sensation is bolstered by a fairly high acidity. It's best served just a bit cooler.

Rating: 91

Nagano, Japan

MARUSHIN MASAMUNE
"GIN NO MAI"
Junmai ginjō-shu

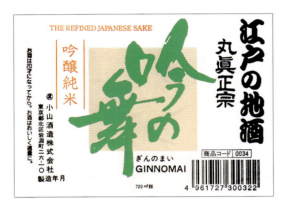

This *kura* has the distinction of being the only saké brewery remaining in the twenty-three wards comprising the city of Tokyo, although there are others in the suburbs that comprise greater Tokyo.

Overall: A soft flavor profile with a dry touch initially, moving to reveal a sweetness lurking in the background.

Rating: 83

Tokyo, Japan

MASUIZUMI

Junmai daiginjō-shu

A tremendous blend of fine flavor and good, *ginjō-shu* fragrance. The fragrance is full and sensual, reminiscent of apples. A rich, clear, but full flavor with a rice-like touch and a nice tickle to the tongue complete the package.

Overall: A truly great saké to get to know and help wean yourself off the wine habit. It's not inexpensive, but is a true value. Avoid warming; it's best served a bit colder than most saké, not too cold but well below room temperature.

Rating: 94

Toyama, Japan

MASUMI

"SAN-KA"

Junmai daiginjō-shu

Light and airy, with a fairly pronounced flowery fragrance and supporting fruit essence; a rather wine-like saké; crisp and clean flavor throughout, with a slightly long but refined and crisp tail. Masumi products are known for their mellowness and stability—any one of them is well worth drinking.

Overall: Another good saké with which to attempt the transition from wine.

Rating: 93

Nagano, Japan

MIYOZAKURA

"KI-IPPON"

Junmai-shu

Rather unobtrusive and balanced flavor, with no particular aspect standing out too much; mellow and almost effervescent fragrance, slightly citrus-like and a bit milky at the same time.

Overall: A mature saké, settled and deep. It's more expressive at room temperature, although warming may not be the best choice.

Rating: 84

Gifu, Japan

MIZUBASHO

Junmai-shu

A few years ago, the young president here made a decision to step up to the plate, modernize the brewery, and brew better *ginjō-shu*. Now, the company even exports to the United States. Clear and just a little soft on the palate, with a slight grainy mouth feel; slight tones of vegetation in the background as well.

Overall: Mizubasho is light and only mildly distinctive; saké about which one cannot complain.

Rating: 83

Gumma, Japan

Momo no Shizuku

Junmai ginjō-shu

A very faint, melon-like fragrance clears the way for a clean, streamlined flavor. It is very soft, as is to be expected with saké from Fushimi. A decently high acidity is effective in spreading the softness. There is a *junmai daiginjō-shu* version that is more fragrant and lively, particularly in the nose, with a lighter flavor profile.

Overall: This is not a saké with a lot of depth or complexity, but rather refreshingly simple and straightforward.

Rating: 86

Kyoto, Japan

MOMOKAWA
Tokubetsu honjōzō-shu

An interesting flavor profile that seems dry at times and sweeter at others, largely dependent on temperature; mild touch of grapes in the nose. Momokawa started, and is still involved with, the SakéOne brewery in Oregon, reviewed elsewhere herein.

Overall: Friendly and eminently drinkable saké. There's enough acidity to allow this to go well with a wide range of food, including light meat.

Rating: 83

Aomori, Japan

Nanbu Bijin

Junmai ginjō-shu

Typical of saké from the Tohoku region, in northern Japan; a gentle acidity tones down the sweetness and lightens the saké. There is a delicate construction of flavor, a well-defined character of fine-grained complexity that is characteristic not only of this saké, but all of the saké brewed at this *kura*.

Overall: A good, rice-laden flavor, slightly rich and neutral, fragrant but not fruity.

Rating: 85

Iwate, Japan

NISHI NO SEKI

Junmai-shu

A player in the world of premium saké from long ago, Nishi no Seki has been making and selling *ginjō-shu* for decades. Their *junmai-shu*, however, is enough to satisfy, with a slightly astringent nose typical of *junmai-shu*.

Overall: Rich and cocoa-laced, this has a nice sweet richness that also makes it wonderful warmed.

Rating: 87

Oita, Japan

Niwa no Uguisu

"Daruma Label"

Tokubetsu junmai-shu

From a small firm brewing some big saké, this is famous as much for the flavor as for the label, with its picture of a famous Zen monk. A fairly heavy flavor comes out in the center, but the initial impact on the palate is actually quite light and dry; with the after-flavor being fruity and buoyant.

Overall: Nice clean tail that invites one back again and again.

Rating: 86

Fukuoka, Japan

OHYAMA

Tokubetsu junmai-shu

Fragrance is rather mild and subdued, but the body is full, and mouth feel is significant. Generally dry, but a semblance of sweetness comes back into the picture as you continue to sip.

Overall: Stable and solid, like an old friend, with a flavor guaranteed to please. Warming is best avoided, at least with the *junmai-shu* version.

Rating: 85

Yamagata, Japan

OROKU

"KEI"

Ginjō-shu

Although the body is fairly light, the sensation of flavor is, on top of that, fairly heavy; nice flowery and raisin-doused fragrance. This saké also comes in a *nama-zake* version that is a bit spritzier and more fragrant.

Overall: A unique saké with an unforgettable distinction: its heavy, strong, prune-like undertone.

Rating: 92

Shimane, Japan

ŌTEMON

Daiginjō-shu

A soft, rich, and billowing saké, quite fragrant, with peaches and flowers the dominant theme; the full richness is distributed well enough to be unobtrusive, not overpowering. Indeed, it is quite elegant.

Overall: A nice, mature, rounded aspect to this saké ties the rice-like flavors and the fruity remnants into a well-trimmed package.

Rating: 92

Fukuoka, Japan

OTOKOYAMA

"KIMOTO JUNMAI"

Junmai-shu

Long ago, there were saké brands called Otokoyama all over the country, most of them named after one famous *kura* in Nada. Now, only a few remain. This one, in Hokkaido, is easily the most famous. Made with the *kimoto* method, but not nearly as tart as most *kimoto* saké.

Overall: Rather mellow and dry, with some bitterness in the background.

Rating: 83

Hokkaido, Japan

OZEKI

"JŪDAN-SHIKOMI"

Ozeki is the third-largest saké brewer in Japan, with a huge line of products. This may be the most unique. The saké is made by adding the rice to the fermenting mash in ten additions rather than the usual three.

Overall: This very sweet saké is quite interesting as a dessert liquor.

Rating: 79

Hyogo, Japan

Ozeki

Junmai ginjō-shu

Ozeki also has a brewery in the United States, where they are producing a nice *junmai ginjō-shu* with a mild nose of gentle rice flavors, slightly flowery.

Overall: Mild and fairly balanced.

Rating: 75

Hollister, California

REIJIN

Junmai ginjō-shu

Very smooth, with light prune and rice-like flavors in the background. The owner of Reijin puts a lot of time into experimenting with aging saké, and with various yeasts. The results are always interesting, and Reijin offers a wide range of *ko-shu*, or aged saké, as well.

Overall: Slightly dry, and not as soft as most of the saké from the Suwa region of Nagano.

Rating: 84

Nagano, Japan

Rihaku
"Chotokusen"
Junmai ginjō-shu

A saké truly representative of the Shimane region and the Izumo *tōji* who brew there. A rich fragrance, fundamentally nutty, but supported by a gently fruity sweetness to create a unique essence; all Rihaku saké can be trusted to present this same thread of uniqueness and quality.

Overall: The flavor is rich, layered, and deep, but a good healthy acidity keeps it light in nature, with an interesting tartness—easy to drink.

Rating: 94

Shimane, Japan

RIKYUBAI

Junmai ginjō-shu

A lively saké, vibrant and clear. It starts out quietly, with a light fragrance of pears and plums, and a fairly mellow entry to the palate. Later, however, a light and bouncy nature exposes all ranges of flavors, transported nicely by a moderate acidity.

Overall: Solidly constructed yet playful and alive, this saké grows on you very quickly.

Rating: 94

Osaka, Japan

SAKÉONE

"DIAMOND"

Junmai ginjō-shu

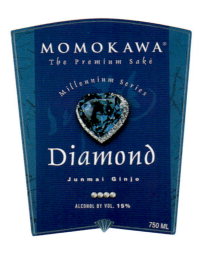

Clean, high-profile United States *ginjō-shu*, with slight pears in the nose, seguing into a crisp, fairly dry flavor; slight bitter notes establish themselves in the background and keep the saké well-grounded.

Overall: Nice when served slightly chilled to just below room temperature.

Rating: 84

Forest Grove, Oregon

SASAICHI

Junmai-shu

A bit of citrus and acidity; tighter flavor than most *junmai-shu*, not as full on the palate and much quieter fragrance.

Overall: Light and easy to appreciate.

Rating: 82

Yamanashi, Japan

Sato no Homare

"Kakunko"

Nama junmai ginjō-shu

Everything made at this tiny *kura* is both *junmai ginjō-shu* (or better) and also *nama-zake*—an amazing feat. This very fragrant saké, with violets and strawberries in a deeply entrenched nose, has light, dancing flavors. With written records that go back 850 years, this *kura* can claim to be the oldest still actively brewing in Japan.

Overall: Very refined and elegant, typical of *nama-zake*. Extremely fragrant.

Rating: 91

Ibaraki, Japan

SAWANOI

Junmai ginjō-shu

Initially, Sawanoi is dry, crisp, and firm, perhaps with a note of grilled corn in the flavor. But soon it spreads out, as if pulled across the palate; perhaps just a trace of earthy bitterness in the background.

Overall: Crisp, clean, and basically dry, but with a softness that comes out, especially when close to room temperature.

Rating: 84

Tokyo, Japan

Sawa no Tsuru

"Zuicho"

Daiginjō-shu

Sawa no Tsuru is the twelfth largest producer in Japan, and was the first large brewer to come out with *ginjō-shu*. Zuicho is unlike their less distinct products, and indeed has a fairly fruity nose, with raisins and figs flickering lightly about. This fruitiness continues into the middle of the flavor profile, which is light and dignified.

Overall: Dry, solid, and satisfying.

Rating: 83

Hyogo, Japan

SEKAI NO HANA

Junmai-shu

Slightly on the sweet side, without the higher acidity expected from a *junmai-shu*; it does, however, exhibit a typical Shimane touch in the nut-like essence of the nose, laced with figs and prunes. A moderate acidity encompasses it all and ties the flavors together.

Overall: Good at room temperature, but will present a simpler face when chilled.

Rating: 83

Shimane, Japan

SHICHIFUKUJIN

Junmai-shu

This has a rich, full, rice-laden flavor that presents a rather cool sensation to the palate. Despite the fact that it is brewed with #9 yeast, there is not a whole lot of fruitiness; more of a dry, settled, rich, and nutty touch evident in the center of the tongue.

Overall: A fairly simple saké, best served just below room temperature, with neither too much warmth nor too much chilling.

Rating: 85

Iwate, Japan

SHIDAIZUMI
Junmai ginjō-shu

This saké, as listed on the label, is also a *muroka* (unfiltered) *nama* (unpasteurized) *genshu* (undiluted saké). Basically, they press it and then bottle it without micro-filtering, pasteurizing, or adding water. This gives rise to a full, rich, zingy flavor with a very lively nose and a bit of roughness.

Overall: Shidaizumi saké is in general soft and seductive, with a feminine richness in the background, and mild fruity fragrances.

Rating: 88

Shizuoka, Japan

SHIGEMASU

Junmai ginjō-shu

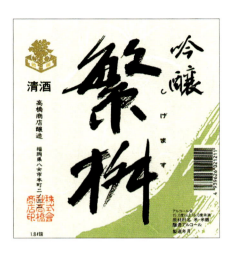

An interesting combination of contrasting flavors; somewhat dry and spicy flavor changes into a richer, more buttery tone, then fades back to dry; moderate flowery nose is tied in closely with the flavor; good consistency of product.

Overall: A saké that will stand on its own, without food, if necessary; this is good at room temperature or chilled.

Rating: 89

Fukuoka, Japan

SHIMEHARITZURU

"JUN"

Junmai ginjō-shu

A fairly well known Niigata saké, with a smooth and soft flavor, beyond being simply light and dry. Ample mouth feel and low acid flavors give this a bit more body than average. Shimeharitzuru has more refined and fragrant versions, such as "Gold Label" *Daiginjō-shu*, that are worth both the search and the money.

Overall: Perhaps the best of the Niigata sakés.

Rating: 90

Niigata, Japan

SHINKAME

"HIKOMAGO"

Junmai daiginjō-shu

Shinkame is a small brewery that does things its own way. Everything here is *junmai-shu*, and aged much longer before shipping than at most *kura*. Although light and refined, this *daiginjō-shu* has a strong earth and bitter/astringent line that many may not prefer. It may be the best saké on the planet for warming.

Overall: Who says you can't warm good saké? This is unbelievably wonderful when heated gently.

Rating: 90

Saitama, Japan

SHIRATAKI
"JOZEN MIZU NO GOTOSHI"

Shirataki gives names to its saké, but refuses to assign them to a class like *junmai-shu* or *ginjō-shu*. The company believes they should sell on their flavor, not their classification. And sell they do. A noticeable anise touch to the thick fragrance melds into a creamy flavor profile, dry and crisp, suffused with vanilla.

Overall: A popular saké with a moderately clean finish.

Rating: 84

Niigata, Japan

SHIRAYUKI

Junmai-shu

Mild, barely perceptible, citrus-laced nose; fairly stalwart flavor, quite a bit on the sweet side, heavy and friendly.

Overall: Not a bad choice for warming.

Rating: 78

Hyogo, Japan

SHOCHIKUBAI
Ginjō-shu

Rather dry, with a nice fruity essence, and light palate; somewhat grainy mouth feel makes it pleasant to drink with simpler food. Shochikubai is the fourth largest brewer in Japan, a very well known name with a massive array of saké products available everywhere.

Overall: This is nice chilled. Warming may not bring out its best.

Rating: 75

Berkeley, California

SHUTENDŌJI

Junmai-shu

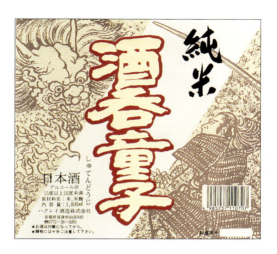

Fairly soft up front, but with flavor lined with herbal or even mineral traces and a soft, slightly acidic finish. Best served neither overly chilled nor any warmer than room temperature; this fairly narrow range seems to allow the nature of this saké to most easily shine through.

Overall: Nice combination of a full, rich *junmai-shu* with a clean but vivid mouth feel, and a light, clean overall saké style for which Shutendōji is known.

Rating: 86

Kyoto, Japan

SUEHIRO

"GENSAI"

Daiginjō-shu

Usually a purveyor of typical Fukushima soft styles, Suehiro has stepped a bit out of character with this saké. Well-entrenched, earthy flavors; mild fragrance. Most Suehiro is very soft and seductive, worth searching for if that is what you like.

Overall: A fairly strong impact, bolstered by higher-than-usual alcohol content.

Rating: 86

Fukushima, Japan

SUIGEI

Junmai ginjō-shu

Suigei means "drunken whale." The fragrance is faint but rice-like, a bit reminiscent of cinnamon. It's a typical Kochi saké in that it is very dry, but with an underlying richness; the quickly evaporating finish leaves your palate wanting more.

Overall: Quite clean on the palate, with few off-flavors, but not devoid of character.

Rating: 89

Kochi, Japan

SUISHIN

Tokubetsu junmai-shu

Quite distinctive; the nose is reminiscent of freshly steamed rice, with not much fruit or flowers; flavor is quite light, and the softness of the water is supplanted by a significant acid presence notable in every aspect of the flavor.

Overall: Clean and smooth throughout.

Rating: 82

Hiroshima, Japan

SUWAIZUMI

"MANTENSEI"

Junmai ginjō-shu

An interesting, somewhat different *junmai-shu*; rice-like flavor with a slight chestnut touch in the background; the fragrance, too, is more floral than average. Suwaizumi also make a wonderful *daiginjō-shu* called Ōtori that is worth searching for.

Overall: Lighter and younger in feel than most *junmai-shu*, with not nearly the acidity or heaviness that most have.

Rating: 87

Tottori, Japan

SUMINOE
Junmai ginjō-shu

A gently sweet saké, soft and demure; not for those who like powerful, in-your-face saké. Understated nose reminiscent of flowers and rich earth, with a mellow, absorbing mouth feel. More than anything else, Suminoe has an intuitive quality to it, wherein you sip it and think, "Wow, that's good," about ten seconds later.

Overall: Fascinating and wonderful, best just slightly chilled.

Rating: 92

Miyagi, Japan

TAKAISAMI
Tokubetsu junmai-shu

First and foremost, Takaisami, or "bravery of the hawk," has presence. Almost ignoring trends, the bitter and astringent elements of this saké bounce off the perfectly gauged acidity to provide a solid canvas upon which other flavors can be expressed.

Overall: Highly recommended; well rounded and mature; be sure to experiment with various temperatures as the saké will change greatly at each.

Rating: 94

Tottori, Japan

TAKASAGO

Ginjō-shu

Brewed with relatively soft water flowing down from Mt. Fuji and filtering through the layers of rock, this has an overall smooth feeling; just a bit on the sweet side, with a fairly full flavor that spreads quickly due to a nice high acid content.

Overall: Smooth, dry, and solid, with a subdued fragrance, Takasago works quite well with food.

Rating: 89

Shizuoka, Japan

TAKASHIMIZU
Ginjō-shu

Takashimizu is one of Japan's top twenty brewers in terms of volume. As such, a lot of what they make is inexpensive saké with minimal character. However, their higher grade saké tend to be truly outstanding, balanced to the core. Gentle fruit flavors dance just below the viscous surface; a well grounded, mildly fruity nose that does not fade.

Overall: Light on the palate, with an airy, grainy mouth feel.

Rating: 89

Akita, Japan

TAKI NO KOI
"KITSUI"
Junmai ginjō-shu

This is a mellow, low-key saké typical of the old and settled Nada style, from a tiny brewer in this region of huge breweries. A quiet and barely perceptible nose, but with a warming, slightly tarrish, vegetation-laced flavor; nice acidity and mouth feel.

Overall: Great slightly chilled, better at room temperature, and good warmed as well.

Rating: 88

Hyogo, Japan

TAMANOHIKARI
Junmai ginjō-shu

A quintessentially Kyoto saké. Soft, sweet, and feminine, charming and absorbing. Very faint rice-like fragrance. The sweetness is balanced nicely by a typical *junmai-shu* high acidity, and beneath that is an astringency tightening the flavors together.

Overall: A mellow richness helps it go well with food; best served at room temperature.

Rating: 83

Kyoto, Japan

TATEYAMA

Junmai ginjō-shu

All saké from Tateyama, one of the top thirty breweries in Japan, is very drinkable; slightly soft and dry, with a rice-like fragrance rather than a fruity or flowery nose; a bitter note in the background provides a somewhat earthy touch.

Overall: Nice body that you can almost sink your teeth into, yet a refined facet as well.

Rating: 88

Toyama, Japan

Tatsuriki

"Akitsu"

Junmai daiginjō-shu

In this saké, bitter tones and somewhat vegetation-laced elements play off each other; the acidity hovers in the background, enlivening the other flavors. Mellow and settled, the almost intuitive richness comes out of the background.

Overall: A bit of exposure to air, such as decanting, does this saké good. It's best at room temperature or chilled.

Rating: 93

Hyogo, Japan

TEDORIGAWA
"JUNMAI GOLD"
Junmai-shu

A quiet, rice-esque nose and a full, fairly dry flavor with lively oases of flavor arising here and there across the profile; fairly crisp on the tongue at first, softening and mellowing along the way. Tedorigawa makes several other *ginjō-shu*, as well as a *daiginjō-shu* called "Meiryū"; all are outstanding saké and outstanding values.

Overall: Not a bad choice to try gently warmed; the name Tedorigawa will never fail to satisfy.

Rating: 90

Ishikawa, Japan

TENGUMAI

Junmai-shu

A rich and astringent, almost earthy nose that deeply penetrates and reveals the sturdy acidity of the saké to come; as with all Tengumai products, the tail is lively, almost springing away from your tongue. This is still light, for Tengumai, which makes a number of *yamahai-shikomi* products that are even stronger in flavor.

Overall: Quite a unique flavor, with bitter and acidic factions playing off each other nicely, and woody and oily tones in the background.

Rating: 88

Ishikawa, Japan

TENJU

Junmai-shu

Typical of regional style with a tight, rather than fat, flavor profile, Tenju has a light, almost transparent sweetness with a pleasing, if simple, rice fragrance. The initial softness is supported by very light acidity in the flavor, creating the added nuance of crispness. Tenju also makes an ultra-premium, rather expensive saké called Chōkai, which is worth the search and the price.

Overall: An extension of all the good things about saké from this region, with nothing overdone.

Rating: 87

Akita, Japan

Tentaka

"Kokoro"

Junmai ginjō-shu

The moderate fragrance is touched with a bit of greenery, but slightly flowery on top of that. The acid content is fairly high but it gets buried—in a good way—within the other encompassing aspects of the flavor profile.

Overall: A clean and crisp saké, with a flavor that, while not excessively dry, is very solidly constructed.

Rating: 89

Tochigi, Japan

TENZAN
"HOTARU-GAWA"
Junmai ginjō-shu

A relatively fat, full flavor that hangs out a bit; a fairly low acidity keeps the flavors from running around in your mouth too much, lending a richness that stops just short of being cloying. Faint peaches in the nose fade into a drier than expected flavor that strikes the palate softly, with a buttery essence rising up later.

Overall: Good at room temperature or slightly chilled. Be open, however, to experimentation.

Rating: 88

Saga, Japan

TOSATZURU

Junmai-shu

Mild, demure nose, with a faint, sweet creaminess; like most saké from Kochi, Tosatzuru is quite dry; earthy tones present themselves after a few seconds; long and acid-bolstered tail that tingles somewhat as it fades away.

Overall: The profile from beginning to end is even and balanced, with no overpowering facets.

Rating: 84

Kochi, Japan

Toyo no Aki

Tokubetsu junmai-shu

Truly elegant saké. A faint fragrance with tones of pecans and hazelnuts. The flavor seems to have a little bit of everything—sweetness, dry elements, a unifying acidity, peach tones, and more, but you have to look for it. Deep and layered.

Overall: Serve at room temperature or even gently warmed. Overchilling would not be wise.

Rating: 89

Shimane, Japan

TSUKASA BOTAN

"SENCHU HASSAKU"

Junmai-shu

The first thing to strike you about this saké, besides the fluorescent orange calligraphy on the label, is the bone-dry flavor. Yet, behind all that is something of substance, a meaty and almost sweet note in the background. The crisp attack on the palate fades with a bit more grace and some softness.

Overall: Bone-dry and light, but satisfying.

Rating: 87

Kochi, Japan

TSUKI NO KATSURA

Junmai ginjō-shu

The sweeter facets bounce around with acidic tones to create a nice balance, delivered in a well-rounded package that is soft in a way typical of Kyoto saké. Tsuki no Katsura also makes a *junmai nigori* saké, that rich, cloudy piña colada of the saké world.

Overall: Soft, with a crispness in the recesses.

Rating: 84

Kyoto, Japan

TSUKI NO WA

Tokubetsu junmai-shu

The name Tsuki no Wa means "ring around the moon;" interesting nose, flowers on top with grass and earth suffusing that; the flavor, especially in the middle part of the palate, has a great graininess to it that is decidedly rice-like.

Overall: A slightly sweet saké, diffused by a thoroughly distributed acidity.

Rating: 88

Iwate, Japan

UGO NO TSUKI

Daiginjō-shu

Soft and reasonably fruity, this is a very delicate saké with great potential for expansiveness as it dances across the palate. A moderate acidity pushes a most interesting nuttiness to the forefront of the flavor profile; exits the palate by absorbing into the tongue, more than passing across the throat.

Overall: As the company is small, this may be hard to find, but it's well worth the search.

Rating: 93

Hiroshima, Japan

Umenishiki
Junmai daiginjō-shu

Umenishiki makes a wide range of saké styles and flavor profiles, and seems to create just about anything they want. This *junmai daiginjō-shu* has a fairly light approach to the palate, but deep in the recesses of this complex saké, a certain heaviness can be sensed.

Overall: A fairly wide but well-tailored flavor, with a nice, prominent floral bouquet.

Rating: 88

Ehime, Japan

UMENOYADO

Junmai ginjō-shu

Well rounded, as it should be after careful aging for two years before shipping; nice bouquet balancing flora and lighter fruity essences; good body and subtle richness with various flavors blooming at different times.

Overall: Although quite nice when chilled, a plethora of flavors awaken just below room temperature, guaranteeing you will never, ever tire of this one.

Rating: 92

Nara, Japan

URAKASUMI

Junmai-shu

One of the original movers and shakers of the *ginjō-shu* boom; mellow fragrance dominated by steamed rice, chestnuts, and acidity; a dry flavor profile that gives rise to a nice second bouquet as you drink.

Overall: A relaxed and mellow flavor, not wildly distinct but consistent and fitting for a great many occasions.

Rating: 87

Miyagi, Japan

WAKATAKE
"ONIKOROSHI"
Junmai-shu

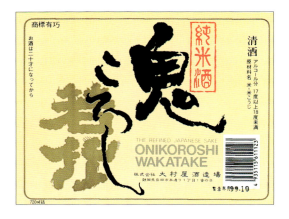

"Onikoroshi" means demon killer. Crisp and clean, with a moderately low acid presence, and a nice, billowing spread across the palate; quite light, with a sweetness lurking in the background, waiting its turn to titillate.

Overall: Clean and crisp, so it may not stand up to strong food. However, it can easily be drunk by itself; best cool or chilled.

Rating: 91

Shizuoka, Japan

WAKATSURU

"KI-IPPON"

Junmai-shu

A solidly-built saké, but with a soft touch at the beginning; slight apples and cantaloupe are seemingly apparent in the beginning, but fade quickly as the flavor becomes drier and firmer; slightly grainy tail will have fans and foes.

Overall: Clean, with few off-flavors, but enough mouth feel to avoid boredom.

Rating: 83

Toyama, Japan

YAEGAKI
"MU"
Junmai ginjō-shu

Fundamentally a dry saké, but with a smooth and refined rice-like flavor on top, robust and full; faint, well-rounded nose with pear notes and a bit of peach, perhaps a bit of greenery too; fairly low acid presence, which allows the flavor to maintain its center-heavy richness.

Overall: A wonderfully settled and calm saké.

Rating: 83

Hyogo, Japan

YAMATOGAWA
"SHUSEIGANKAI"
Junmai ginjō-shu

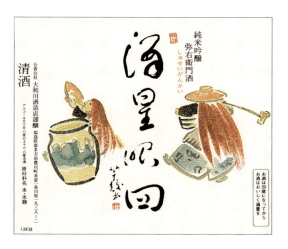

Yamatogawa *junmai-shu* uses a newly developed yeast called by various names, with F-1 being the easiest to remember. This yeast helps bring out more aromatic components during fermentation. The flavor is light and soft, with a clean and grainy rice flavor and slight sweetness.

Overall: Fragrant, light, and soft.

Rating: 89

Fukushima, Japan

YAMATZURU

Junmai daiginjō-shu

Soft, seductive nose that tickles the back of your olfactory senses rather than being overt; nice rice-based fragrance, delicate and fast to fade; the flavor is slightly sweet at first and crystal clear, becoming much drier a few seconds later.

Overall: A simple and narrowly built saké, elegant and light.

Rating: 88

Nara, Japan

YOAKEMAE

"KI-IPPON"

Junmai-shu

Lively, pro-active fragrance that jumps out to meet you, slightly rice-laced but with fruit essences like plum and fig hidden in there as well. Good, thick-boned flavor; soft, demure, and slightly sweet. Yoakemae also makes a wonderful *nama* (unpasteurized) version of this saké which is rich and festive.

Overall: Wonderful slightly chilled on warm evenings.

Rating: 87

Nagano, Japan

YONETSURU

"FORMULA ONE"

Daiginjō-shu

Named for the Formula One race cars, whose slick and speedy image the brewers hoped to emulate in this saké. It has a full fragrance laced with pear and ripe peaches, and somewhat grassy undercurrent. Tail fades quickly, but not so much that you cannot enjoy its passing.

Overall: A gentle, dry, and clean flavor, slightly rice-like and subtly rich in the recesses.

Rating: 88

Yamagata, Japan

Yorokobi no Izumi

"Kyokuchi"

Daiginjō-shu

The "Kyokuchi" saké comes in two varieties: one made with Yamada Nishiki rice, and one made with Ōmachi rice. They are different enough to be considered two entirely different saké. The one referred to here is the Yamada Nishiki version, with floral and honey facets to the settled but omnipresent nose.

Overall: Light in flavor, but with an astoundingly well-structured flavor beneath; solid, clean, and subtly rich.

Rating: 91

Okayama, Japan

Part III

DIRECTORY OF SAKÉ BREWERIES

Notes on the Brewery Names

Kabushiki-gaisha (Incorporated), *Yūgen-gaisha* (Limited), and *Gōshi-gaisha* (conglomerate) all refer to "company." So do *Shoten, Shokai,* and others. They appear here as they do in the formal company name. *Junmai-shu, ginjō* (without the *-shu*), and *daiginjō* (without the *-shu*) are listed as they are used conversationally.

The brand name, or *meigara,* is the first name listed in each entry. Very often each saké under that *meigara* will have a sub-name. For example, Reijin is the *meigara,* and Ginrei is the sub-name. A product with no subname would be Reijin *Junmai-shu.*

Front of 800-year-old Sudo Honke, the oldest active brewery in Japan.

AMANOZAKE

Saijō Gōshi-gaisha

OSAKA, JAPAN

HISTORY

Founded in 1718, this *kura* took its name from a brewery that existed in a temple called Kongōji on Mt. Amano, in the South Kawachi region of Osaka. There, more than seventy monks brewed a slightly darker, heavier ancestor of today's saké. This was the original Amanozake, a favorite of Hideyoshi Toyotomi, one the great unifying warlords of medieval Japan. Brewed with water from a nearby well, all of Amanozake's products have long been cherished in Osaka and Kyoto. In 1972, the company created a saké called *Sōbō-shu*, which is a revival of the original monk-brewed saké of old.

PRODUCTS INCLUDE:

Kamon standard saké; Rei *Junmai-shu*; Kisshō *Ginjō*; Ah *Daiginjō*; Un *Daiginjō*; Ah-Un *Daiginjō*; *Sōbō-shu*

AMERICA PACIFIC RIM

California Ki-Ippon

VERNON, CALIFORNIA

HISTORY

APR is owned and operated by a company comprised of several players (including brewers and distributors) of alcoholic beverages in Japan. Most of what they produce is very reasonably priced, light in flavor, and creatively marketed. Established in 1987, APR also makes fresh, draft saké available only in the Los Angeles area.

PRODUCTS INCLUDE:

California Ki-Ippon *Tokubetsu Junmai-shu;* Arabashiri Nama *Genshu*

CHIYO NO KAME

Kameoka Shuzō Gōshi-gaisha

EHIME, JAPAN

HISTORY

Founded in 1871, this is a tiny but incredible *kura*, whose *tōji* are definitely into doing their own thing. Creative and artistic, nothing here is normal, but all of it is very, very good. The saké ferments in small, 750-kg. tanks. Half of their saké is *junmai ginjō*, half is *shizuku* (only gravity is used to separate the saké from the lees; it is allowed to drip from canvas bags), and almost everything is aged. All of their *ginjō* is *nama-zake*. All of the saké is aged from three to ten years, sometimes even longer, at freezing temperatures. This gives it a well-rounded texture and a settled maturity, while avoiding any musty or old aspects. One product, Ginga Tetsudo, is often served as a saké slush—quite a nice dessert.

PRODUCTS INCLUDE:

Chiyo no Kame Ginga Tetsudo *Junmai Daiginjō*;
Chiyo no Kame Shizuku *Junmai Daiginjō*;
Chiyo no Kame *Junmai-shu*

CHIYO NO SONO

Chiyo no Sono Shuzō Kabushiki-gaisha

KUMAMOTO, JAPAN

HISTORY

During World War II, all saké brewers began to add distilled alcohol to make up for the shortage of rice, and continued to do so after the war ended. Finally, in 1964, Chiyo no Sono made the first postwar *junmai-shu*. At first, they couldn't sell it all, as the public seemed to have forgotten that this was once how all saké was made. But they stuck with it, becoming a key part of the history of premium saké. Now *junmai-shu* is loved by many for its character and solid structure. This *kura* founded the Junsui Nihonshu Kyōkai (Pure Saké Association) in 1973, along with fifteen other brewers, in an effort to return to the roots of saké brewing, and to encourage other brewers to do so as well. Most of this saké is aged a full year before releasing it for sale, giving it an earthy, well-rounded maturity.

PRODUCTS INCLUDE:
Chiyo no Sono *Honjōzō*; Chiyo no Sono Excel *Daiginjō*; Chiyo no Sono Shuhai *Junmai Daiginjō*; Chiyo no Sono Shuhai Mark II *Junmai-shu*

DAISHICHI

Daishichi Shuzō Kabushiki-gaisha

FUKUSHIMA, JAPAN

HISTORY

Daishichi, founded in 1752, is best known for making saké using the *kimoto* method for creating yeast starter. *Kimoto* calls for the *kurabito* (brewers) to stand around the small yeast starter vat and create a liquid paste of the rice and *kōji* by ramming long poles into the mixture for hours. Exhausting, to say the least, it also takes twice as long (up to a month) as the other, more common, method. It does, however, create a saké of more distinction, with varying degrees of an almost sweet, tart, and acidic flavor. Seventy percent of the saké made here is *kimoto*. Daishichi also produced the first *kimoto daiginjō*. Most of the saké here is soft, with a slight overall sweetness. It is aged a bit longer than many others, and pays off with a rounded, mellow flavor.

PRODUCTS INCLUDE:
Daishichi standard saké; Daishichi *Junmai-shu*; Daishichi Kyokujō *Junmai Daiginjō*; Daishichi Hiden *Junmai Ginjō*; Daishichi Kimoto *Honjōzō*

DEWAZAKURA

Dewazakura Shuzō Kabushiki-gaisha

YAMAGATA, JAPAN

HISTORY

Named for the lovely *sakura* (cherry blossoms) on nearby Mount Maitzuru, Dewazakura has been producing local saké since 1891. It is local in the sense that rice grown locally is used, and it is brewed by a *tōji* and staff from the immediate region, unlike the seasonal traveling craftsmen employed by most *kura*. Brewing here is a mixture of labor-intensive technique and modern technology. For example, to ensure that the brewers are fully in touch with the condition of the steamed rice, it is carried in burlap cloths, not transported by air hose. This also keeps the kernels from getting crushed too early. All aging tanks are jacket-cooled with coolant, so that a great deal of saké can be stored and shipped in its unpasteurized state. In short, Dewazakura combines the best of old and new.

PRODUCTS INCLUDE:

Haru no Awayuki *Nigori-zaké*; Dewazakura Ikkō *Junmai-shu*; Dewazakura Ōka *Ginjō*; Dewazakura *Daiginjō*

ECHIGŌ TSURUKAME

Uehara Shuzō Kabushiki-gaisha

NIIGATA, JAPAN

HISTORY

Founded in 1888, the company's name refers to the old name for Niigata (Echigō) and the characters for crane and turtle, two symbols of long life and good fortune. The current president made his way back to the family business after studying Italian art history and enrolling in an acting school in Rome. Upon returning to

Japan, he was not content with simply brewing saké, but wanted to try his hand at micro-brewed beer. Although many saké breweries have taken on this side business, Uehara Shuzō applied for and received the very first license to do so in Japan. Overall, the saké here is dry and clean, with a soft touch and some acidity. The beer tends to be the same way.

PRODUCTS INCLUDE:
Echigō Tsurukame standard saké; Echigō *Honjōzō*; Echigō *Daiginjō*; Echigō *Junmai Daiginjō*

GEKKEIKAN

Gekkeikan Kabushiki-gaisha

KYOTO, JAPAN

HISTORY

Gekkeikan is the biggest saké producer in the world. Founded in 1637, it was known until the end of the nineteenth century as Tama no Izumi. Its contributions to the industry are countless: it was the first to use glass bottles, the first to brew year round, and the first to use rice liquefiers. Gekkeikan has at least six breweries. One of them, the Kanzukuri *kura*, has six *tōji*, each from a different school and region, who compete with each other to brew the best saké. The company has also opened a brewery in California. Indeed, despite the immediate bias often taken toward large brewers and big business, Gekkeikan brews some very good saké. Gekkeikan, which generally wins at least one gold medal each year, has won six awards—one for each *kura*—in 1991, 1992, and 1996.

PRODUCTS INCLUDE:

Gekkeikan has countless varieties of saké, several in each category, available in all sizes and shapes, with seasonal and experimental products as well.

HAKKAISAN

Hakkaisan Shuzō Kabushiki-gaisha

NIIGATA, JAPAN

HISTORY

In the late 1970s and early 1980s, when the *ginjō* boom hit Japan, Niigata saké was at the center of it all. And Hakkaisan, founded in 1922, was one of those Niigata saké that received plenty of accolades. Named after one of the three great mountains of Echigo (old Niigata), Mount Hakkai, it kept production small and grew only as much as necessary. As such, its products can be hard to find, but are worth the search for those fond of the style. Like much Niigata saké, Hakkaisan is dry, but the water used in brewing, which filters through the mountains, gives it a wonderful smoothness. The company's motto is "making saké is making *ginjō*," and all its saké gets *ginjō*-like attention. In 1989, it built a large underground storage area, ideal for aging saké.

PRODUCTS INCLUDE:

Hakkaisan *Honjōzō*; Hakkaisan *Junmai Ginjō*; Hakkaisan *Daiginjō*

HAKUTSURU

Hakutsuru Shuzō Kabushiki-gaisha

HYOGO, JAPAN

HISTORY

Hakutsuru is the largest brewer in Nada, which is the largest and most significant brewing area in all of Japan. However, it is still second in size to Gekkeikan of Kyoto. Established in 1743 from an existing lumber company, it took the name Hakutsuru, or "white crane," four years later. *Tsuru* (crane) is the most common character in Japanese saké names, but it was first used here.

Hakutsuru's saké is a bit lighter than most from the Nada region, yet it has more flavor impact.

PRODUCTS INCLUDE:
Hakutsuru has a huge product line, with products in every class and price range.

HAKUSAN

Kohnan, Inc.

NAPA, CALIFORNIA

HISTORY
Owned not by a saké brewery, but by a soft-drink affiliate in Japan, Hakusan does benefit from the presence of several on-site brewing personnel sent over from Japan. Nice graphic design and a cool brewery in the heart of California wine country give the brand great appeal. Experimental and active marketing ensures it continues to improve its saké, which has been brewed since 1989.

PRODUCTS INCLUDE:
Hakusan Saké; Hakusan Premium Saké; Hakusan Mild (Draft) Saké

HARUSHIKA

Kabushiki-gaisha Imanishi Seibei Shōten

NARA, JAPAN

HISTORY
Founded in 1903, this brewery used to make the saké offered up at nearby Kasuga Daishi, an important Shinto shrine. The name, which means "spring deer," is actually an abbreviation of a longer phrase referring to

this illustrious past. Seventy percent of the saké brewed here is *junmai-shu*. The water for brewing, and the water used later for bringing the alcohol content down, come from two different sources. The *Cho-karakuchi Junmai-shu* listed below is actively being exported to the United States and elsewhere.

PRODUCTS INCLUDE:
Harushika *Honjōzō*; Harushika *Junmai-shu*; Harushika *Chōkarakuchi Junmai-shu*; Harushika *Daiginjō*

JŪYONDAI

Takagi Shuzō Kabushiki-gaisha

YAMAGATA, JAPAN

HISTORY
This is quite possibly the most popular saké in Japan right now, and well deserving of that title and status. Admirably, Jūyondai refuses to increase production or price—which is great, assuming you find a bottle. It is widely available in saké pubs and restaurants, but not at retail stores. Although the *kura* was established in 1681, this brand name did not come into use until several years ago. Jūyondai means "fourteenth generation," as the current president is the fourteenth successive owner.

PRODUCTS INCLUDE:
Jūyondai Honmaru *Honjōzō*; Jūyondai Nakadori *Junmai-shu*; Jūyondai *Junmai Ginjō*

KAIUN

Kabushiki-gaisha Doi Shuzō-jō

SHIZUOKA, JAPAN

HISTORY

Kaiun, or "beckoning of good fortune," has been brewing here since 1871, four years after the Meiji Restoration, when the local village leader decided a career change was called for. He named his new saké Kaiun in hopes for growth for the village. Water is brought from a spring near the grounds of an ancient castle where many battles had been fought. It is fairly "mysterious" water in that it is quite soft, which usually means that fermentation will be slow, but this water causes a lively, vigorous ferment. On top of that, it requires no filtering or fermentation-aiding chemical adjustments, and the final saké does not need to be charcoal-filtered. All the saké here is light and elegant. The brewers have long been active in making Shizuoka saké as good as it can be, and have even developed their own yeast (HD-1).

PRODUCTS INCLUDE:

Kaiun Iwai-saké *Honjōzō*; Kaiun *Junmai Ginjō*; Kaiun *Daiginjō*

KAMOIZUMI

Kamoizumi Shuzō Kabushiki-gaisha

HIROSHIMA, JAPAN

HISTORY

Kamoizumi has a style all its own. Although located in the center of Saijō, the brewing village in Hiroshima that has more saké brewers in less space than all but a handful of other locales in Japan, its saké is not typical of the region. Founded in 1911, this *kura* is probably best known for its Ryokusen saké, and the amber color that gives it an irresistible appeal. Rather than being sweet or dry, its rich and almost heavy—but not cloying—flavors do well at all temperatures. The owners are fun-loving and energetic, and put as much into keeping the culture around saké alive as they do into brewing it.

PRODUCTS INCLUDE:
Kamoizumi Ryokusen Honshikomi *Junmai Daiginjō*; Kamoizumi Niji no Uta *Junmai Daiginjō*; Kamoizumi Kotobuki *Daiginjō*

KENBISHI

Kenbishi Shuzō Kabushiki-gaisha

HYOGO, JAPAN

HISTORY

Founded sometime between 1504 and 1521 (the actual date is not clear) in the Itami region, then famous for saké, Kenbishi eventually moved to Nada with its great water flowing down Mount Rokko. It is the eleventh largest brewer in Japan, with eight *kura* spread out across the region, and ten *tōji* among them. Despite the fact that Kenbishi is technically a "mass producer," several years back its brewers began to make all their *kōji* in small trays, ensuring temperature and quality. They also make all *moto* yeast starters by the *yamahai* method. All tanks are fermented at low temperatures for about thirty days. These are techniques usually reserved for only the best saké. The company is fairly secretive about its products and methods of brewing and business. Tours, for example, are not permitted.

PRODUCTS INCLUDE:

Kenbishi only makes the four products listed below, the last of which is an aged saké.

Kenbishi *Honjōzō*; Kuromatsu Kenbishi *Honjōzō*; Kyokujō Kuromatsu Kenbishi *Honjōzō*; Kuromatsu Kenbishi Zuisho *Junmai-shu*

KIYOIZUMI

Kusumi Shuzō Kabushiki-gaisha

NIIGATA, JAPAN

HISTORY

In 1981, the president of this brewery had eleven hundred grains of a strain of rice extinct except for that handful of seeds. Slowly and carefully, he grew what he could from them. Known as Kame no Ō, it was a rice he had heard about from his *tōji*, who had heard about it when he was young. Eventually, enough was grown to brew saké. This romantic story soon led to a comic book series and a television drama. Kiyoizumi was founded in 1833, named after the clear spring on the mountain behind the brewery. The brewers still maintain a close alliance with local rice farmers and the network of retailers handling their products. While of healthy size, Kiyoizumi maintains a small, family-run, *"jizake"* feeling.

PRODUCTS INCLUDE:
Kiyoizumi *Honjōzō*; Kiyoizumi *Tokubetsu Junmai-shu*; Kiyoizumi Kame no Ō *Daiginjō*

KOKURYŪ

Kokuryū Shuzō

FUKUI, JAPAN

HISTORY

The name Kokuryū means "black dragon;" the name was taken from the name of a local river when the *kura* was established in 1804. The name of the river has since changed to the Kokuryū-gawa, or Nine-headed Dragon River. It is still from this fast-flowing river that the water for brewing is extracted. Kokuryū has enjoyed immense popularity over the last few years, and deservingly so. Kokuryū always seems to be one notch of distinction ahead of most of its peers in any given grade of saké. They produce a lot of very expensive, hard-to-find saké, often some of which is drip-pressed and wonderful, but it is not necessary to go that far. Their reasonably priced, medium grade saké are certainly memorable enough.

PRODUCTS INCLUDE:

Kokuryū *Honjōzō*; Kokuryū *Daiginjō*; Kokuryū "Ryu" *Daiginjō*; Kokuryū Shizuku *Junmai Daiginjō*

KŌRO

Kabushiki-gaisha Kumamoto-ken Shuzō Kenkyūjō

KUMAMOTO, JAPAN

HISTORY

This *kura* was founded in 1909 with money from all the other *kura* in the prefecture, with the purpose of experimenting with and improving the quality of the saké in that region. It eventually became a company in its own right in 1918, but only after isolating the most widely used *ginjō* yeast for saké, known as #9, or alternatively, Kumamoto yeast. Kōro also developed a commonly used system for ventilation of the room used to make *kōji*. The company remains dedicated to developments that will help make better saké, not just in Kumamoto, but everywhere. Along the way, it is making some great, unique saké, fruity and light.

PRODUCTS INCLUDE:

Kōro Tokusen *Honjōzō*; Kōro *Junmai-Ginjō*; Kōro *Daiginjō*

KOSHI NO KANBAI

Ishimoto Shuzō Kabushiki-gaisha

NIIGATA, JAPAN

HISTORY

This is perhaps the most esteemed name among Japan's saké brewers. When *jizake*, saké from smaller brewers in the countryside, became popular in the early 1980s, it was this brewery that led the way. The *tanrei karakuchi* (light and dry) style was a favorite among connoisseurs, and remains so with many today. Although the company has increased production and is now quite large, it can still be hard to find premium Koshi no Kanbai—it is that popular. Rumor has it that the local Niigata people still like to serve this saké warm, despite its premium status.

PRODUCTS INCLUDE:

Koshi no Kanbai standard saké; Koshi no Kanbai *Honjōzō*; Koshi no Kanbai *Tokubetsu Honjōzō*; Koshi no Kanbai *Junmai Ginjō*; Koshi no Kanbai *Daiginjō*

KOTSUTSUMI

Kabushiki-gaisha Nishiyama Shuzō-jō

HYOGO, JAPAN

HISTORY

Brewing in Hyogo since 1849, Kotsutsumi produces saké that is a bit different from the expected Hyogo style. It is one of the most consistent saké on the market, and one of the most intuitive—you almost feel, rather than taste, its wonderfulness. Two generations ago, the president was a haiku student whose teacher, a famous poet, assigned the saké's name, meaning "small drum." Kotsutsumi has a modernist graphic designer who has given a slick, angular look to all its labels, making them instantly recognizable. On the brewing side, all its *kōji* is made by hand, and the brewers are fond of using yeast #10, which is fairly rare in the Kansai region of western Japan, as it is much more of a Tohoku, or northern Japanese, yeast.

PRODUCTS INCLUDE:
Kotsutsumi *Junmai-shu*; Kotsutsumi Shusen *Ginjō*; Kotsutsumi Tenraku *Daiginjō*

MABOROSHI

Nakaō Jōzō Kabushiki-gaisha

HIROSHIMA, JAPAN

HISTORY

The main brand name of this *kura* is Seikyō, whose characters mean "sincerity" and "mirror." A fairly loose but wonderfully poetic translation of the company's stated meaning behind the name is "at the end of the day, the brewers can look in the mirror and know they made the best saké they could." Located in Hiroshima, brewing with water from the great Kamo River, they create *moto* yeast starter in a unique way, giving the Maboroshi saké a distinctive green apple touch. The Maboroshi line of *ginjō* and *daiginjō* are wonderfully balanced, fragrant, and full of rice-laden flavor, while being somewhat light overall.

PRODUCTS INCLUDE:
Seikyō *Junmai-shu*; Seikyō Tenshi no Saké *Ginjō*; Maboroshi *Ginjō*; Maboroshi *Daiginjō*

MADO NO UME

Mado no Ume Shuzō Kabushiki-gaisha

SAGA, JAPAN

HISTORY

Although the *kura* was established in 1688, in 1860 the branch of a plum tree *(ume)* snaked in through the window *(mado)*, and a blossom dropped into a tank of saké. That saké ended up being fragrant and wonderful. This prompted the local samurai lord to speak words of praise, and the name Mado no Ume was taken from his utterances. Mado no Ume makes a wide range of saké styles, from aged saké to *yamahai-shikomi*, and light saké styles as well. Long-term consistency and all-around pleasant flavor make this saké worth remembering.

PRODUCTS INCLUDE:

Mado no Ume standard saké; Mado no Ume *Honjōzō*; Mado no Ume *Junmai-shu*; Mado no Ume Kaden *Ginjō*; Mado no Ume Kōbai *Daiginjō*

MAIHIME

Maihime Shuzō Kabushiki-gaisha

NAGANO, JAPAN

HISTORY

Maihime means "dancing princess," and the name is taken from an old nineteenth century novel. After this brewery began making saké by that name, a second novel with the same title was written by another author. The characters for Maihime on the label of the *ginjō* were taken from a letter written by the author of that book, Yasunari Kawabata, to the brewery. The saké is brewed by a Nagano native, a *tōji* of the Suwa school. The water used in brewing flows down from Mount Kirigamine, one of the highest peaks in the area, and is filtered slowly through the rocky layers. It's a very stable saké from year to year, mildly fruity and fairly soft.

PRODUCTS INCLUDE:
Maihime standard saké; Maihime *Honjōzō*; Maihime Karakuchi Ki-ippon *Junmai-shu*; Maihime *Junmai Ginjō*

MARUSHIN MASAMUNE

Koyama Shuten Kabushiki-gaisha

TOKYO, JAPAN

HISTORY

This is the only remaining *sakagura* within the twenty-three wards of Tokyo, where it has been since 1878. There are others in the greater metropolitan area, but none can claim to be within the city limits. One might think it would be hard to get good water for saké brewing in a metropolis the size of Tokyo, but in 1941, Marushin Masamune dug a 130-meter deep well that picks up water flowing through the rocks of the Chichubu mountains to the north. This water has nearly the same chemical makeup as Miyamizu, the water flowing down from Mount Rokko in Kobe, which made Nada so famous a brewing spot.

PRODUCTS INCLUDE:

Marushin Masamune standard saké; Marushin *Honjōzō*; Marushin *Junmai-shu*; Marushin *Daiginjō*; Marushin *Junmai Daiginjō*

MASUMI

Miyasaka Shuzō Kabushiki-gaisha

NAGANO, JAPAN

HISTORY

Founded in 1662, this is one of the most significant and important breweries in Japan. In 1946, Masumi took the top three prizes in the government tastings called the Seishu Kanpyōkai (a now defunct contest, for saké laid to mellow for six months or so). It also won the Shinshu Kanpyōkai, which is a contest for just-brewed saké. The secrets behind Masumi's success are fine water, fine brewers, and a particular yeast, now the most commonly used strain in saké brewing, known as Association #7 Yeast. Masumi identified it, used it, and later helped distribute it across the country. In 1982, it opened a second brewery near the first, which has the distinction of being the highest (in terms of elevation) *sakagura* in Japan. Masumi's standard saké is mellow and clean, appealing to almost everyone. Its higher grades are more fruity and fragrant, but again, almost no one dislikes them. It is all too easy to drink this saké, so be careful!

PRODUCTS INCLUDE:

Masumi Kaden Tzukuri *Tokubetsu Honjōzō*; Masumi Okuden Kan-tzukuri *Junmai-shu*; Masumi *Yamahai Shikomi Junmai-shu*; Masumi Yumedono *Junmai Daiginjō*

OTOKOYAMA

Otokoyama Kabushiki-gaisha

HOKKAIDO, JAPAN

HISTORY

Centuries ago, there was a well-known saké in the Itami saké-brewing region near Osaka called Otokoyama. It was enjoyed both in Edo (present-day Tokyo) as well as among the Kyoto court nobles. Hoping to ride on the success of that name, breweries all around the country borrowed the Otokoyama moniker. Today, the Hokkaido Otokoyama is by far the most popular. In 1967, the company moved from the center of town in Asahikawa to the suburbs, where the water used for brewing is filtered through the local mountains. The saké is, in general, dry and refined.

PRODUCTS INCLUDE:

Otokoyama makes a wide range of products, some of which are listed below.

Otokoyama standard saké; Otokoyama *Tokubetsu Junmai-shu*; Otokoyama *Junmai Daiginjō*; Otokoyama Kimoto *Junmai-shu*

OZEKI

Ozeki Kabushiki-gaisha

HYOGO, JAPAN

HISTORY

Ozeki is the third largest brewer in Japan, with operations in the United States as well. Founded in 1711, it became successful under the brand name Manryō, one of several companies in Nada that shipped their casks up to Edo (present-day Tokyo) in ships that constantly went back and forth on saké runs. In 1889, the company changed its name to Ozeki, which was then the highest rank in Sumo wrestling. (Unfortunately for Ozeki, Sumo added a rank higher than Ozeki in the early 1900s.). Ozeki has always been very strong in their marketing strategy and new product development. It opened the first bottling plant in 1924, and was the first to introduce single-size servings, in particular the Ozeki "One Cup." One such product is the Jūdan Shikomi, a very sweet dessert saké made with ten ·additions of rice instead of the usual three. Ozeki even has its own saké research center.

PRODUCTS INCLUDE:
Ozeki makes a vast array of products, some of which are listed below.

Ozeki Karatanba *Honjōzō*; Ozeki Osakaya Chobei *Daiginjō*; Ozeki Jūdan Shikomi *Ginjō*

RIHAKU

Rihaku Shuzō Kabushiki-gaisha

SHIMANE, JAPAN

HISTORY

This *kura* was founded in 1882, although it was not until 1928 that the name Rihaku was adopted. Rihaku was a famous Chinese wandering poet, known in English as Li Po, who lived from 701 to 762. He was known as a kind, open-minded man, famous for drinking a great deal before writing. He is said to have observed, "I drink one large bottle, and I write 100 poems." This *kura* makes lavish use of Rihaku's poems and phrases in its promotional material and labels. Several of its saké are named with phrases from the great poet's words. Rihaku saké is mellow and well-rounded, with a nutty undertone and good acidity.

PRODUCTS INCLUDE:
Rihaku Ryōnin Taishaku *Junmai Ginjō*; Rihaku *Tokubetsu Junmai-shu*; Rihaku *Junmai Daiginjō*

SATO NO HOMARE

Sudo Honke

IBARAKI, JAPAN

HISTORY

This amazing *kura* has the distinction of being the oldest active saké brewery in Japan, at least based on written brewing records dating back to 1141. The current president is the fifty-fourth in succession. Although it is small, the *kura* produces nothing but top-grade saké, all of which is both *junmai* and *nama*, and all of which is *ginjō* class or higher. The company's proprietary yeast gives its saké a wonderful lively fragrance and smooth flavor, as well as a potent second fragrance that arises as you exhale (called a *fukumi-ka*). Recently, it revived a very old rice, found in ancient ruins, and is brewing some saké with that as a way of reviving history.

PRODUCTS INCLUDE:

Sato no Homare Yusura *Junmai Ginjō*; Sato no Homare Kakunko *Junmai Daiginjō*; Sato no Homare Sansensōmoku *Junmai Ginjō*

SAWA NO TSURU

Sawa no Tsuru Shuzō Kabushiki-gaisha

HYOGO, JAPAN

HISTORY

Founded in 1717, this is one of the ten largest brewers in Japan, with three facilities in the heart of the Nada district of Kobe city in Hyogo Prefecture, the saké-brewing capital of the world. Nada saké is known for being fairly masculine in flavor and feel. It is crisp and dry, with little fragrance. Sawa no Tsuru was one of the first Nada *kura* to come out with *ginjō-shu*. The historic original *kura* building was destroyed in the 1995 Great

Hanshin earthquake, but an exact replica was rebuilt and converted into a wonderful *sakagura* museum. Old tools and brewing scenes illustrate the steps of the brewing process, accompanied by videos in Japanese and English. It is a must-visit for anyone passing through Kobe.

PRODUCTS INCLUDE:
Sawa no Tsuru makes countless products, a few of which are listed below.

Sawa no Tsuru Jōsen *Honjōzō*; Sawa no Tsuru Kimoto *Junmai-shu*; Sawa no Tsuru Zuichō *Ginjō*

SHINKAME

Shinkame Shuzō Kabushiki-gaisha

SAITAMA, JAPAN

HISTORY
They do things their own way at Shinkame, which was established in 1848. For one, all the saké is *junmai-shu*. It is also aged for a minimum of two years before shipping, which gives it a certain maturity that allows the company president to state with confidence (and correctly so) that all Shinkame saké can be enjoyed warm as well as cool. The saké is brewed in small amounts, with six *kurabito* to do the work, so it gets a lot of attention. That makes it special. It may not be to everyone's taste, but those who love Shinkame cherish it for its uniqueness.

PRODUCTS INCLUDE:
Shinkame *Junmai-shu*; Hikomago *Junmai-shu*; Hikomago *Junmai Ginjō*; Hikomago *Junmai Daiginjō*

SHIRAYUKI

Onishi Shuzō Kabushiki-gaisha

HYOGO, JAPAN

HISTORY

Although the *kura* was founded in 1550, it was not until 1635 that the name Shirayuki was used. The second-generation owner glimpsed snow atop Mount Fuji as his ship of saké casks bound for Edo passed, inspiring him to rename his product Shirayuki, or "white snow." It is now the seventh largest brewer in Japan, a powerful company that recalls its rich history with the ancient *kura* building that stands in front of the head office. Although it does maintain a brewery in Nada, the region of Kobe that produces a third of Japan's saké, there are four Shirayuki breweries in the even older brewing town of Itami, further north in Hyogo. Its saké is a bit different from the typical product of the region, being softer and less crisp.

PRODUCTS INCLUDE:

As it is a very large brewing company, Shirayuki produces many different saké.

SHŌCHIKUBAI

Takara Shuzō Kabushiki-gaisha

KYOTO, JAPAN

HISTORY

The fourth largest brewer in Japan, Shōchikubai was established in 1832, and is known for brewing all manner of alcoholic products, including *mirin* (saké used in cooking) and *shōchū* (a distilled spirit). The name Shōchikubai refers to pine, bamboo, and plum, which have represented an auspicious symbol in Japan for centuries. The company opened a brewery in the United

States in 1982 in Berkeley, California, and is currently America's largest saké brewer.

PRODUCTS INCLUDE:
Products brewed in the United States include:
Shōchikubai Regular; Shōchikubai Extra-Dry; Shōchikubai Premium *Ginjō, Nigori,* and *Nama*

Products brewed in Japan include:
Shōchikubai standard saké; Shōchikubai *Daiginjō;* Shōchikubai *Junmai daiginjō;* Shōchikubai Chōtokusen *Junmai-shu;* Shōchikubai Jōsen *Honjōzō*

SHUTENDŌJI

Hakurei Shuzō Kabushiki-gaisha

KYOTO, JAPAN

HISTORY

Although this *kura* also produces a saké called Hakurei, it is perhaps better known for the Shutendōji, named for a band of thieves that lived in the Ōe Mountains near Kyoto more than a thousand years ago. They were wiped out by a famous group of noble warriors, but continued to grow in mystique as generations passed, in order to exaggerate the strength and prowess of the noble warriors. Eventually, the Shutendōji became supernatural demons called Oni. The company, established in 1832, concentrates its effort on making lots of *yamahai-shikomi* saké, which generally has a fuller, sturdier flavor profile.

PRODUCTS INCLUDE:
Shutendōji *Honjōzō;* Shutendōji Tango-moto-tzukuri *Junmai-shu;* Hakugin no Shizuku *Ginjō*

SUIGEI

Suigei Shuzō Kabushiki-gaisha

KOCHI, JAPAN

HISTORY

The name Suigei means "drunken whale," which seems a suitably amusing name for a saké. However, it was actually taken from the written words of a local politician, Yodo Yamanouchi, when the *kura* was founded in 1882. Yamanouchi was instrumental in the Meiji restoration, which returned power to the Emperor in 1868. Sixty percent of the saké here is *ginjō*. Four types of rice are used, and some grades of saké contain all four. Since everything else is the same for any given grade, in terms of brewing steps like rice polishing and *kōji* making, it is possible to compare the different qualities of the four rice types themselves. Naturally, this is only one aspect of what Suigei does, for it has many other established, reliable products.

PRODUCTS INCLUDE:

Suigei *Tokubetsu Honjōzō*; Suigei *Tokubetsu Junmai-shu*; Suigei *Junmai Ginjō*; Suigei *Junmai Daiginjō*

TAKASHIMIZU

Akita Shurui Seizō Kabushiki-gaisha

AKITA, JAPAN

HISTORY

In 1944, no less than twenty-four small saké breweries joined to become Takashimizu. Before long, twelve dropped out, and the present manifestation of Takashimizu is made up of the remaining dozen. They dispensed with all of the former *meigara* (brand names), and took a vote on a new one. Takashimizu, which can be loosely translated as "pure water from on high," was the clear winner. The company is committed to continually improving its saké. Its motto is, "Let all of our customers be our salesmen." Although Takashimizu is the largest brewer in eastern Japan, its quality standards are extremely high, and the saké is, overall, wonderful.

PRODUCTS INCLUDE:
Takashimizu Seisen standard saké; Takashimizu *Tokubetsu Junmai-shu*; Takashimizu Zuichō *Daiginjō*

TAKI NO KOI

Kimura Shuzō Kabushiki-gaisha

HYOGO, JAPAN

HISTORY

Founded in the Kobe brewing center of Nada back in 1758, Taki no Koi is one of the tiny breweries that sits among giants. The name is taken from a Chinese myth in which a carp climbs up a waterfall and is transformed into a dragon. The brewery has survived wars, earthquakes, and other catastrophes that have decimated most of the area's other small *kura* over the decades. The company motto is, "To brew Nada-esque saké as a Nada *jizake* brewer should." Taki no Koi's product is indeed worthy of the distinction of Nada saké. It is brewed with the water historically known as Miyamizu, which flows through the nearby Rokko mountains and rises up in wells. Miyamizu contains the perfect saké-brewing mineral content.

PRODUCTS INCLUDE:
Taki no Koi *Honjōzō*; Taki no Koi *Junmai Ginjō*; Taki no Koi *Daiginjō*; Taki no Koi Kissui *Junmai Ginjō*

TAMA NO HIKARI

Tama no Hikari Shuzō Kabushiki-gaisha

KYOTO, JAPAN

HISTORY

This is one of the classic large Kyoto brewers, founded in 1673. After World War II, it relocated to the Fushimi region of Kyoto, as did many other brewers, for the superior water. Today, the company operates three different breweries. In the early 1960s, it seriously began to promote a return to pure saké, and immediately ceased the use of all additives. The emphasis is very strongly on *junmai-shu*, as almost all of what is produced is free of added alcohol. About non-*junmai* saké, Tama no Hikari's president has commented, "It may be good, but it isn't real *nihonshu*." A relatively large portion of the saké is brewed with organically grown rice.

PRODUCTS INCLUDE:

Tama no Hikari makes a vast array of products, which include:

Tama no Hikari Saka-damashi *Junmai Ginjō*; Tama no Hikari Yamada Nishiki 100% *Junmai Ginjō*; Tama no Hikari Bizen Ōmachi 100% *Junmai Daiginjō*

TENGUMAI

Kabushiki-gaisha Shata Shuzō

ISHIKAWA, JAPAN

HISTORY

At the time this *kura* was founded in 1823, the sound of a drum was heard in a nearby forest. It was presumed to come from long-nosed, demonic, mythical creatures called Tengu, dancing the night away. This was the inspiration for the name Tengumai, or "dance of the

Tengu." This company brews a lot of unusual and memorable saké. A significant portion is brewed with the *yamahai-shikomi* method, and somewhat stronger-flavored *yamahai* than that produced by most other brewers. Many Tengumai saké are suitable for warming. The company also brings a good amount of aged saké to the market. It is rich and strong, but definitely not for everyone.

PRODUCTS INCLUDE:
Tengumai Yawara *Junmai-shu*; Tengumai *Yamahai-shikomi Junmai-shu*; Tengumai *Ginjō*; Tengumai *Ko-ko-shu* (aged saké)

TENTAKA

Tentaka Shuzō Kabushiki-gaisha

TOCHIGI, JAPAN

HISTORY

The founder of this *kura* had a dream during a trip to Kyoto in which he saw a hawk soaring toward the heavens. The hawk is a powerful image, with its piercing eyes and ability to fly high. When, in 1914, he bought a brewery in Tochigi prefecture that was near bankruptcy, the dream remained in his memory, and he decided to sell his saké under the name Tentaka, or "Soaring Hawk." The Tentaka brewery sits deep in the countryside, surrounded by rice fields and mountains, in an area of few tourists. The founder based his philosophy on the notion that, "If it isn't dry, it isn't saké." Tentaka's products remain so today, though they exhibit plenty of diversity and character. The "Kokoro" saké has been a strong seller for perhaps thirty years.

PRODUCTS INCLUDE:
Tentaka Kiyomatsu standard saké; Tentaka Kokoro *Junmai Ginjō-shu*; Tentaka Ginshō *Junmai Daiginjō*

TOSATZURU

Tosa Shuzō Kabushiki-gaisha

KOCHI, JAPAN

HISTORY

Tosatzuru adapts the old name for this region, Tosa, where everyone, from average citizens to nobility, is known for the ability to drink a lot. There is still a belief among saké pub proprietors that if a customer can walk home straight, you weren't a good host. Not surprisingly, saké from the Tosa region is dry. Although Tosatzuru is now the thirtieth largest brewery in the country, it began as a lumber company that shipped regularly to Edo, or present-day Tokyo. Eventually, the owners realized that shipping saké would be more profitable, and brewing began in 1845.

PRODUCTS INCLUDE:

Tosatzuru makes a large number of products, some of which are listed below.

Tosatzuru standard saké; Tosatzuru *Honjōzō*; Tosatzuru *Junmai-shu*; Tosatzuru *Ginjō*; Tosatzuru *Junmai Daiginjō*; Tosatzuru Hakuhō *Daiginjō*

TSUKASA BOTAN

Tsukasa Botan Shuzō Kabushiki-gaisha

KOCHI, JAPAN

HISTORY

Tsukasa Botan is brewed in the southern part of what used to be known as the Tosa region, amidst the scenic beauty of the town of Sakawa. It dates back 1603, and along the way has been the favorite saké of many significant figures in Japanese history. The current name, in fact, was taken from the complimentary words of a former Imperial Minister late in the nineteenth century:

"The botan (peony) is the king of all flowers, and this botan is the top of the botans." In his book *Ryoma Ga Yuku*, the famous author Ryotaro Shiba writes, "In Sakawa of the Tosa region, the saké that is the top of botans is being brewed. The people of Tosa love this kind of dry saké, and after drinking a bottle and a half, a faint sweetness eventually comes out in the center of the flavor, and you can just keep drinking."

PRODUCTS INCLUDE:
Tsukasa Botan Senchu Hassaku *Junmai-shu*; Tsukasa Botan Deluxe *Daiginjō*; Tsukasa Botan Shizuku *Daiginjō*

UME NO YADO

Ume no Yado Shuzō Kabushiki-gaisha

NARA, JAPAN

HISTORY

Founded in 1888, the company takes its name from the words "plum tree lodgings." Long ago, a nightingale lived in a plum tree in the *kura* garden. The nightingale is long gone, but both the 360-year old tree and the name remain. Working here is an Englishman named Philip Harper, the only non-Japanese *kurabito* in the country. He helps brew saké that is prized by connoisseurs all over Japan. From the standard saké on up, the finest rice, water, and craftsmanship are evident in the flavor and nose.

PRODUCTS INCLUDE:
Ume no Yado *Honjōzō*; Ume no Yado Kōbai *Junmai Ginjō*; Ume no Yado Yamada Nishiki *Junmai Daiginjō*; Ume no Yado Ōmachi *Junmai Daiginjō*

WAKATAKE ONIKOROSHI

Omuraya Shuzōjō

SHIZUOKA, JAPAN

HISTORY

The name Onikoroshi means "demon killer." Originally, it was used to refer to a saké that was so bad it would kill a demon. But over time, it took on the opposite meaning, and came to refer to a saké that is so damn *good* it would kill a demon. Countless saké brewed in Japan use the name Onikoroshi, but Wakatake Onikoroshi is certainly a cut above the rest. Long ago, many travelers passed through the Shizuoka town of Shimada, situated between Tokyo and Kyoto. There were many saké brewers back then, but now only this one remains, brewing as it has been since 1832. The *daiginjō* is called Onna-nakase, or "make the ladies cry."

PRODUCTS INCLUDE:

Wakatake Onikorishi *Honjōzō*; Wakatake Onikorishi *Junmai-shu*; Wakatake Onna-nakase *Junmai Daiginjō*

WAKATSURU

Wakatsuru Shuzō Kabushiki-gaisha

TOYAMA, JAPAN

HISTORY

Wakatsuru means "young crane." More saké names use the character for crane than any other, because it is considered auspicious. This company tries to brew saké that is "like a young crane, dancing in the sky." There are actually two *kura* comprising this brewery, which was established in 1861, and each has its own *tōji*. What is interesting, however, is that they are from different regions and brewing schools. This leads to disparate saké styles, which provides Wakatsuru saké with great diversity.

PRODUCTS INCLUDE:
Wakatsuru standard saké; Wakatsura *Honjōzō*; Wakatsura *Junmai Daiginjō*; Wakatsuru Kissui *Junmai Ginjō*; Wakatsuru Soshin *Daiginjō*

RESOURCES

Since saké continues to grow in popularity in the United States, the number of saké shops and saké pubs is constantly growing; the list below is only a small sample. A more updated list of saké shops and organizations, as well as a list of saké pubs in the United States, can always be found at www.saké-world.com.

Retail Stores

CALIFORNIA

Ebisu Market
18930-40 Brookhurst St.
Fountain Valley, CA 92708
Tel: (714)962-2108

Jana Market
1099 Reganti Dr.
Concord, CA 94518
Tel: (925)682-0422

Marukai
1740 W Artesia Blvd.
Gardena, CA 90248
Tel: (310)660-6300

Maruwa Foods
1737 Post St.
San Fransico, CA 94115
Tel: (415)563-1901

Mitsuwa Asian Supermarket
665 Paularino Ave.
Costa Mesa, CA 92626
Tel: (714)557-6699

Mitsuwa Asian Supermarket
333 S Alameda St.
Los Angelos, CA 90013
Tel: (213)687-6699

Mitsuwa Asian Supermarket
3760 Centinela Ave.
Los Angelos, CA 90066
Tel: (310)398-2113

Mitsuwa Asian Supermarket
4240 Kearney Mesa Rd. #119
San Diego, CA 92111
Tel: (858)569-6699

Mitsuwa Asian Supermarket
675 Saratoga Ave.
San Jose, CA 95129
Tel: (408)255-6690

Mitsuwa Asian Supermarket
21515 Western Ave.
Torrance, CA 90501
Tel: (310)782-0335

Resources

Mitsuwa Market Place
515 W Las Tunas Dr.
San Gabriel, CA 91776
Tel: (626)457-2899

Nijiya Market
17869 Colima Rd.
City of Industry, CA 91784
Tel: (626)913-9991

Nijiya Market
143 E El Camino Real
Mountain View, CA 94040
Tel: (650)691-1600

Nijiya Market
3860 Convoy St. #121
San Deigo, CA 92111
Tel: (858)268-3821

Nijiya Market
2121 W 182nd St.
Torrance, CA 90504
Tel: (310)366-7200

Nijiya Market
2533-B Pacific Coast Hwy.
Torrance, CA 90505
Tel: (310)534-3000

Nijiya Market
2130 Sawtelle Blvd. #105
West Los Angelos, CA 90025
Tel: (310)575-3300

Nippon Foods
2935 W Ball Rd.
Anaheim, CA 92804
Tel: (714)826-5321

Pacific Supermarket
1620 W Rendondo Beach Blvd.
Gardenia, CA 90247
Tel: (310)323-7696

Santo Market
245 E Taylor St.
San Jose, CA 95112
Tel: (408)295-5406

Tokyo Fish Market
1220 San Pablo Ave.
Berkley, CA 94760
Tel: (602)968-1890

Uoki K. Sakai
1656 Post St.
San Fransico, CA 94115
Tel: (415)921-0514

Yaoya-San
10566 San Pablo Ave.
El Cerrita, CA 94530
Tel: (510)526-7444

COLORADO

Applejack Liquor
320 Youngfield St.
Wheatridge, CO 80033
Tel: (303)233-3331

Liquor Mart
1750 15th St.
Boulder, CO 80302
Tel: (303)449-3374

Lukus Liquor
8457 S Yosemite
Littleton, CO 80124
Tel: (303)792-2288

HAWAII

Marukai
2310 Kamehameha Hwy.
Honolulu, HI 96819
Tel: (808)845-5051

Daiei
801 Kaheka St.
Honolulu, HI 96814
Tel: (808)973-4800

ILLINOIS

Mitsuwa Asain Supermarket
100 E. Algonquin Rd.
Arlington Heights, IL 60005
Tel: (847)956-6699

Sam's
1720 N Marcey St.
Chicago, IL 60614
Tel: (312)664-4394

MICHIGAN

One World Market
42705-B Grand River Ave.
Novi, MI 48375
Tel: (248)374-0844

NEVADA

Japan Food Express
4001 S Decatuor Blvd. #17
Las Vegas, NV 89103
Tel: (702)737-0881

NEW JERSEY

Mitsuwa Asian Supermarket
595 River Rd.
Edgewater, NJ 07020
Tel: (201)941-9113

NEW YORK

Ambassador Wines and Spirits
1020 2nd Ave.
New York, NY 10022
Tel: (212)421-5078

Beekman Liquors
500 Lexington Ave.
New York, NY 10017
Tel: (212)759-5857

Embassy Wines and Spirits
796 Lexington Ave
New York, NY 10021
Tel: (212)838-6551

McCabes Wine and Spirits
1347 3rd Ave.
New York, NY 10021
Tel: (212)737-0790

Park Avenue Liquor Shop
292 Madison Ave.
New York, NY 10017
Tel: (212)685-2442

OHIO

Jungle Jim's
5440 Dixie Hwy.
Fairfield, OH 45014
Tel: (513)829-1918

Koyama Shoten
5857 Sawmill Rd.
Dublin, OH 43717
Tel: (614)761-8118

OREGON

Uwajimaya
10500 SW Beaverton-Hillsdale Hwy.
Beaverton, OR 97005
Tel: (503)643-4512

Anzen
736 NE Martin Luther King Blvd.
Portland, OR 97232
Tel: (503)233-5111

TEXAS

Danny's Liquor
2001 W Northwest Hwy. #120
Dallas, TX 75220
Tel: (972)556-0148

Monticello Liquor
4855 N Central
Dallas, TX 75205
Tel: (214)520-6618

Nippon Daido
11138 Westheimer Rd.
Houston, TX 77042
Tel: (713)785-0815

VIRGINIA

Naniwa Foods
6730 Curran St.
McLean, VA 02247
Tel: (703)893-7209

WASHINGTON

Larry's Market
699 120th Ave. NE
Bellevue, WA 98005
Tel: (425)453-0600

Larry's Market
12321 120th Place NE
Kirkland, WA 98034
Tel: (425)820-2300

Larry's Market
10008 Aurora Ave. N
Seattle, WA 98133
Tel: (206)527-5333

Uwajimaya
15555 NE 24th St.
Bellevue, WA 98007
Tel: (425)747-9012

CANADA

Barrique Wine Imports
439 Wellington St. W
Suite 106
Toronto
ONT M5V 1E7
Tel: (416)598-0033

Featherstone and Company
435-B Berry St.
Winnipeg
MAN R3J 1N6
Tel: (204)837-6874

Kado Enterprises
1938 Deanhome Rd.
Mississauga
ONT L5J 2K4
Tel: (905)822-1340

Liquid Art Fine Wines
2233 Burrard St.
Vancouver
BC V6J 3H9
Tel: (604)713-0841

Promark Sourcing
Chesterfield Pl. #F15
North Vancouver
BC V7M 3K3
Tel: (604)904-5171

Organizations

Japan Prestige Saké Association
100 Vandam St.
New York, NY 10013
Tel: (212)924-8189

JFC International
540 Forbes Blvd.
South San Francisco, CA 94080
Tel: (650)871-1660

Mutual Trading Company
New York: 25 Knickerbocker Rd.
Moonachie, NJ 07074
Tel: (201)933-9555
Los Angeles: 431 Crocker St.
Los Angeles, CA 90013
Tel: (213)626-9458

SakéOne Corporation
820 Elm Street
Forest Grove, OR 97116
Tel: (503)357-7056

Saké Service Institute Inc.
377 Manhattan Ave., Suite 2R
Brooklyn, NY 11211
Tel: (718)349-7179

Wine of Japan Import, Inc.
235 West Parkway
Pompton Plains, NJ 07444
Tel: (973)835-8585

English-language Saké Websites

Chemistry of Saké Brewing
http://www.gekkeikan-saké.com/

eSaké Homepage
www.esaké.com

Hakusan Saké Gardens
http://.hakusan.com/

How to Homebrew Saké
http://brewery.org/brewery/library/saké_MH0796.html

Izumibashi
http://www.sphere.ad.jp/izmibasi/

Japan Central Brewers Union Homepage
www.japansaké.or.jp/saké/english/index.html

The Joy of Saké
http://www.joyofsaké.com/

Rich Webb's Guide to Saké Production
http://home1.gte.net/richwebb/saképrod.html

Saké Association of America
http://www.sakéusa.com/saké/index.html

Saké Direct
http://saké-direct.com/

Saké Kingdom
http://manzoku.topica.ne.jp/saké/index_e.html

Saké Labels
http://ecbos.tmit.ac.jp/saké/label.html

Saké Merchandise
http://www.japanesegifts.com/adishes.asp

SakéOne
http://www.sakéone.com

Saké Resource Center
http://www.sakés.com

Saké World
http://www.saké-world.com

Suihitsu
http://suihitsu.co.jp/eng/

Sun Masamune Brewery
http://www.sun-masamune.com.au

Tamanohikari
http://www.saké.com

Umenoyado Brewery Site
http://www.umenoyado.com

GLOSSARY

AMAKUCHI: Sweet-flavored saké.

DAIGINJŌ-SHU: Saké made with rice milled to at least fifty percent and with a small amount of distilled alcohol added to the mash. Brewed using traditional, labor-intensive techniques; flavor is clean, delicate, and complex; represents the pinnacle of the brewer's craft.

FUNA-SHIBORI: A method of pressing saké from the lees by filling meter-long canvas bags with *moromi*, laying them in a large wooden box (*fune*), and cranking the lid down into the box to squeeze out the saké.

FUNE: A large box, usually made of wood or lined with stainless steel, into which canvas bags filled with *moromi* are placed and squeezed to separate saké from the lees in the *funa-shibori* method.

FUTSUU-SHU: "Regular" saké; saké which does not qualify for a special designation.

GENSHU: Undiluted saké which is sold at its naturally occurring strength of about twenty percent alcohol.

GINJŌ-SHU: Saké made with rice milled to at least sixty percent and with a small amount of refined alcohol added to the mash; flavor is light, complex, and delicate.

GO-MI: Five flavors of a saké, consisting of *karami* (dryness), *amami* (sweetness), *nigami* (bitterness), *sanmi* (acidity), and *shibumi* (somewhere between astringency and tartness). The quality of a saké often is assessed by how well these five flavors are in balance.

GUINOMI: Large, artistic saké cups.

HI-OCHI: A condition befalling *nama-zake* that has not been kept cold, so that it therefore turns milky in color, and sweet-tart and yeasty in flavor and aroma.

HIYA-OROSHI: A pasteurization process much like *nama-chozō*, except that the saké is pasteurized before the six month storage period instead of after it (unlike traditionally pasteurized saké, which is processed twice). *Hiya-oroshi* saké is usually released in the fall.

HONJŌZŌ-SHU: Classification for saké made with rice milled to at least seventy percent and with a small amount of refined alcohol added to the mash; generally the flavor is lighter and more fragrant than regular saké.

JIZAKE: Local saké; a "micro-brew;" generally implying a saké which is not mass produced.

JŌSŌ: The step in the brewing process in which the *moromi* is passed through mesh to separate the clear saké and the unfermented solids.

JUNMAI-SHU: Classification for saké made with rice milled to at least seventy percent, and with distilled alcohol added to the brewing process; its flavor is rich, full, and acidic.

JUNMAI DAIGINJŌ-SHU: Classification for saké made with rice milled to at least fifty percent and to which no distilled alcohol has been added; the flavor is clean, delicate, and complex. This saké represents the pinnacle of the brewer's craft.

JUNMAI GINJŌ-SHU: Classification for saké made with rice milled to at least sixty percent and to which no distilled alcohol has been added; the flavor is light, complex, and delicate.

KAMI-DANA: A small Shinto shrine, often found in Japanese homes. A *kami-dana* for *Matsuo-sama*, a Shinto deity related to saké-brewing, is found in every saké brewery.

KANSA: Professional saké tasters maintained by the tax department in Japan who assess saké in government sponsored competitions.

KARAKUCHI: Dry saké.

KASU: The white lees pressed off during *jōsō*.

KIJŌSHU: Fortified saké in which some of the brewing water has been replaced with already-brewed saké.

KIMOTO: A centuries-old, labor-intensive technique for creating the *moto* yeast starter mash which leads to saké with a rich, gamy flavor profile.

KŌJI: Rice onto which *kōji-kin* has been propagated.

KŌJI-KIN: *Aspergillus oryzae*, a mold that creates enzymes that break starch molecules in the rice into fermentable and non-fermentable sugar molecules.

KO-SHU: Aged saké.

KŌTEKIMAI: A term referring to all the varieties of saké rice.

KUCHI-ATARI: The way a saké initially strikes the palate.

KURA: Saké brewery.

KURABITO: A saké brewery worker.

KURAMOTO: The president or other family representative of a saké brewery.

LEES: The unfermented solids left over in a tank of fermenting saké.

MASU: Small wooden box which is one of the traditional vessels from which saké is consumed; it remains a symbol of saké drinking even today.

MEIGARA: Brand name of a saké, found on the label.

MOROMI: Fermenting mash of rice, water, *kōji*, and yeast which yields saké.

MOTO: Yeast starter, or seed mash.

NAMA-CHOZŌ: Pasteurization process in which a saké is stored for about six months, then pasteurized once before shipping, rather than the customary pasteurization process wherein a saké is treated twice.

NAMA-ZAKE: Unpasteurized saké which must be kept refrigerated.

NIGORI-ZAKE: Cloudy saké.

NIHONSHU: Japanese term for saké.

NIHONSHU-DO: See Saké Meter Value.

O-CHOKKO: Small saké cups.

RŌKA: Filtration of remaining solids after the completion of *jōsō*.

SAKAGURA: A saké brewery.

SAKAMAI: Term for varieties of saké rice in the everyday language of the *kura*.

SAKÉ METER VALUE (SMV): Known in Japanese as

nihonshu-do, SMV is the measure of the specific gravity of the saké or the density in comparison to pure water. SMV gives a very loose indication of sweet versus dry; the lower the number, the sweeter the saké.

SEIMAI: Rice polishing (milling).

SEIMAI-BUAI: The percentage of the original size of the grain that remains after rice is milled.

SEISHU: Official legal Japanese name for saké, differentiating it from other alcoholic beverages. Often written on saké labels.

SHIBORI-TATE: Just brewed and pressed saké.

SHINPAKU: Opaque white center of the rice grain of very good saké rice.

SHUBŌ: Yeast starter, or seed mash, for a batch of saké.

SHUZŌ KŌTEKIMAI: A term referring to the varieties of saké rice.

TANREI-KARAKUCHI: Light and dry flavor.

TŌBIN-GAKOI: Saké that was separated into 18-liter bottles *(tōbin)* upon pressing; usually produced by *funa-shibori* or *shizuku* methods.

TŌJI: Head brewer at a *kura.*

TŌJI RYŪHA: Regional group from which a *tōji,* or head brewer, originated.

TOKKURI: Saké flask.

TOKUBETSU HONJŌZŌ-SHU: *Honjōzō-shu* brewed in a special manner, usually with high quality rice or above average polishing.

TOKUBETSU JUNMAI-SHU: *Junmai-shu* brewed in a special manner, usually with high quality rice or above average polishing.

UMAMI: A flavor component related to a hard-to-pinpoint deliciousness.

YAMAHAI SHIKOMI: A centuries-old, labor-intensive technique for creating the *moto* yeast starter mash that, similar to the *kimoto* method, yields saké with a fuller, gamier flavor profile.

Photography and Illustration Credits

© Chiyo no Sono Shuzō: p. 8

© John Gauntner: pp. 23 (bottom left), 29 (bottom left), 34 (top, bottom)

Illustrations © Eiko Nishida; cooltiger@pop07.odn.ne.jp: pp. 42-45

Author photo on jacket flap courtesy of *Savour* Magazine (Tokyo)

Courtesy of Sudo Honke: p. 198

© Tentaka Shuzō: p. 15, 29 (top left, right)

© Takasago Shuzō: pp. 23 (top left, right),

© 2000 Michael Weiss: front and back cover, pp. 2, 6

INDEX

Index